The Inspiring Life of Eudora Welty

Richelle Putnam

Richelle Putnam

Illustrations by John Aycock

Charleston · London

The History Press

Published by The History Press
Charleston, SC 29403
www.historypress.net

Copyright © 2014 by Richelle Putnam
All rights reserved

Cover art by John Aycock

First published 2014

Manufactured in Canada

ISBN 978.1.62619.000.9

Library of Congress CIP data applied for.

Notice: The information in this book is true and complete to the best of our knowledge. It is offered without guarantee on the part of the author or The History Press. The author and The History Press disclaim all liability in connection with the use of this book.

All rights reserved. No part of this book may be reproduced or transmitted in any form whatsoever without prior written permission from the publisher except in the case of brief quotations embodied in critical articles and reviews.

Contents

Introduction	5
Prologue	7
1. Chessie and Chris: Leaving the Past	17
2. Jackson, Mississippi: Forging Ahead	25
3. Early Childhood: Imagination	33
4. World War I: Curiosity	41
5. Segregation: Discovery	53
6. Roaring Twenties: Expression	59
7. High School: Breaking Away	67
8. Flappers and Jazz: Transformation	77
9. College Years: The Journey	87
10. WPA, the Depression and World War II: Destination	99
Epilogue	115
Timeline	123
Learn More About Eudora Welty	127
Notes	131
Collected Works	139
About the Author	143

Introduction

Eudora Welty never strayed from her childhood dream of one day becoming an author. By the age of ten, she was a published writer, and her writing and artwork had won national awards. From there, her writing life took her through war, a depression, the civil rights movement and the deaths of her parents and siblings. Known all over the world as one of America's most important writers, Eudora Welty's roots remained firmly planted at her childhood home of Jackson, Mississippi, where she did what she loved doing most—wrote stories.

Prologue

Rain fell steadily in Jackson the last week of April 1973, threatening to spoil the annual Mississippi Arts Festival. The festival celebrated artists from all over the state. This year, its special honoree was Eudora Welty, and May 2 would become "Eudora Welty Day." One thousand members throughout Mississippi made up the committee whose mission was to honor and commemorate Eudora's accomplishments.[1]

At the end of February, Eudora had returned to Jackson from Mobile with writer friend Reynolds Price. The two writers met in the early spring of 1955. Eudora's train arrived about two o'clock in the morning at the railroad station in Durham, North Carolina. She would speak to the students at Duke that day. Eudora insisted that no one meet her at the station at such an atrocious hour. She could manage getting herself and her bags to her hotel. However, Eudora was the only passenger to step off the train at an unlit, deserted station. Standing alone in the darkness in a strange place, she noticed a lone figure emerge. It came toward her.

"I'm Reynolds Price, a student at Duke," the figure said. He had waited for her train, knowing her destined plight.

She stayed in Durham three days while giving her lecture, "Place in Fiction," at the Woman's College at Duke. During her time

Prologue

there, Eudora read the "only serious short story" Reynolds had ever written. Then she asked him, "May I show this to my agent?" Reynolds was a twenty-two-year-old novice writer. Eudora was a forty-five-year-old master of words. They became lifelong friends. He would be one of many.[2]

Upon her return to Jackson from Mobile with Reynolds, Eudora focused on the coming festival and working with the committee. As much as everyone looked forward to the festival, Jackson was an unsettled environment. Sadly, the 1960s had left Eudora heartbroken. Her mother died on January 20, 1966. Four days later, her brother Edward died from a brain infection. Her other brother, Walter, passed away in January 1959. Eudora's only family left was Walter's wife, Mittie, and their two daughters, Elizabeth and Mary Alice.

With the turbulent 1960s came the demand for equal rights throughout the country. Malcolm X advocated black power. Martin Luther King Jr. dreamed that "one day…former slaves and the sons of former slave owners will be able to sit down together at the table of brotherhood." Even so, Jim Crow remained the law in the South. Despite the Supreme Court's 1954 ruling, the South continued to resist school desegregation. Restaurants like Woolworth's five-and-dime refused to serve blacks at the whites-only counters. In December 1960, the Supreme Court declared segregation illegal. When the Kennedy administration failed to enforce the law, interracial groups of Freedom Riders traveled on buses across the South. This action forced the federal government to step in.

In 1962, after much violent opposition by whites, the all-white University of Mississippi finally enrolled James Meredith, who had been refused admission three times. Alabama made the nation's headlines with its Children's Crusade in Birmingham, labeled the "worst big city in the U.S.A." On September 15, 1963, a member of the Ku Klux Klan set off a bomb at the African American Sixteenth Street Baptist Church in Birmingham. The bomb killed four young girls and injured twenty-two others. In November, in Dallas, Texas, Lee Harvey Oswald assassinated President John F. Kennedy. Ninety-nine minutes later, Vice President Lyndon Baines Johnson took the oath for the presidency on Air Force One.[3]

Prologue

On June 12, 1963, Byron de la Beckwith shot Medgar Evers, field secretary for the National Association for the Advancement of Colored People, outside his home in Jackson, Mississippi. Angered by the news, Eudora wrote a story about the murder titled "Where Is the Voice Coming From." She sent it to William Maxwell, editor at the *New Yorker*. He immediately bought it and rushed it into print. When authorities arrested Beckwith for the murder, too many of Eudora's details about the murder were accurate. To avoid a libel suit, Eudora and the editors changed details of the story over the telephone.[4] After "Where Is the Voice Coming From?" was published, a newspaper reporter called Eudora and asked if anybody had burned a cross on her lawn. She answered, "The people who burn crosses on lawns don't read me in the *New Yorker*."[5]

All-white Millsaps College closed its public events to African Americans in 1958. The college also discouraged its professors from speaking at Tougaloo College, the private, historically black college founded by the American Missionary Association in 1869 in Jackson. However, Eudora and friend Jane Reid Petty could not be hindered. They and others continued to carpool to Tougaloo. Often, they changed vehicles so the sheriff's department wouldn't notice a pattern in their visits and try to stop them.

On April 2, 1963, Millsaps turned away a Tougaloo professor and several students trying to attend a play on the college's campus. Sixteen days later, Eudora Welty gave her address at the Southern Literary Festival, hosted that year by Millsaps College, to an integrated audience, which she requested. After her lecture on "Words into Fiction," she read her story "Powerhouse," about an African American pianist and his band playing at a segregated dance. She made her point.[6]

During the Freedom Summer of '64 in Mississippi, three civil rights workers—Mickey Schwerner, James Chaney and Andrew Goodman—departed Meridian. They traveled to Philadelphia, Mississippi, to check on the black church that the Klan had burned. In Neshoba County, Mississippi, Klansmen ambushed and murdered the three workers. Twenty-one men were accused of the crime. Eighteen were tried. None were convicted of murder. Years later, in 2005, Edgar Ray Killen, a Baptist preacher in Philadelphia, Mississippi, was tried

Prologue

for three counts of murder. He was found guilty on three counts of manslaughter. No one has ever been found guilty of murder in this case.

Congress passed the Civil Rights Act of 1964 prohibiting discrimination based on race in employment, public accommodations, publicly owned facilities, union membership and federally funded programs. In 1967, the Supreme Court ruled that state laws against interracial marriage (called miscegenation) were unconstitutional. President Johnson signed the Civil Rights Act of 1968. That same year, Martin Luther King Jr. and New York senator Robert F. Kennedy were assassinated.

Entering the 1970s, the Vietnam War was the longest and arguably most detested conflict in American history. All over the nation, students protested the Cambodian invasion. National guardsmen killed four protestors at Kent State in Ohio. In Jackson, Mississippi, the police killed two student protestors at Jackson State University.

On January 27 of the year of the Mississippi Arts Festival, U.S. national security adviser Henry Kissinger and North Vietnamese negotiator Le Duc Tho signed the Vietnam War cease-fire. The only stain during the festival would be Watergate and President Nixon's fall from the highest seat in America. The only obstacle would be rain.

While grief, anger and regret accompanied Eudora into the 1970s, recognition through her literary awards and honors were companions. In 1972, President Nixon appointed Eudora to the National Council for the Arts. She received the Gold Medal for the Novel from the National Institute of Arts and Letters. In 1962, Eudora had the honor of presenting William Faulkner, fellow Mississippi author and friend, the Gold Medal for Fiction. Her dear friend Katherine Anne Porter received the same award in 1967. Another Mississippi writer, Tennessee Williams, won the Gold Medal for Drama in 1969.

Eudora provided the Mississippi Arts Festival committee with a list of out-of-town friends to send invitations to for an all-expense-paid visit to celebrate "Eudora Welty Day." Before mailing the invitations, Eudora wrote a personal note on each, explaining why she had provided the committee with their names and addresses. She urged them not to inconvenience themselves on her account.

Acceptances poured in. Reynolds Price immediately replied with a yes. Also attending the festivities was literary critic Mary Lou Aswell,

Prologue

who, in 1941, after working with the *Atlantic Monthly* and *Reader's Digest*, became a fiction editor for *Harper's Bazaar*. She accepted "The Key," the first of Eudora's short stories published in the magazine. Another acceptance came from Nona Balakian. She trained Eudora at the *New York Times Book Review* during Welty's 1944 summer internship. Once she had argued that Eudora, as a writer, "recognized both the region's and human beings' complexities on her own terms."

Another yes came from William Jay Smith, poetry consultant for the Library of Congress, and his wife, Sonja. William—or Bill, as friends called him—was a Rhodes Scholar. Eudora met him in the 1950s while in Florence, Italy, known as the mecca for writers and artists. John Robinson, Eudora's childhood friend and a World War II veteran, had become her first true love interest. He introduced Eudora to the exciting Florence scene frequented by Ralph Ellison, Sinclair Lewis and John Steinbeck. He also introduced her to Bill and Sonja. With them, John and Eudora enjoyed parties, dancing and taking trips together. John Robinson professed his love for Eudora to Bill. He struggled with his love for Eudora like he struggled with homosexuality. This struggle eventually led to the demise of their relationship. John and Eudora remained friends.[7]

An acceptance also arrived from author Katherine Anne Porter, Eudora's mentor and friend. Katherine always believed in Eudora's work.[8]

Ken Millar and his wife, Margaret, also sent their acceptance. Ken and Eudora's relationship was born through letters. Through an April 1970 *New York Times Book Review* interview, Eudora shared her love for mysteries. She confessed that she once wrote a fan letter to crime writer Ross Macdonald (real name Ken Millar). She never mailed it for fear he'd think it "icky."[9] Upon reading this interview, Ken wrote Eudora a fan letter on a beautiful card with a poem entitled "Prayer, Mountaintop Way":

> *Restore all for me in beauty,*
> *Make beautiful all that is before me,*
> *Make beautiful all that is behind me,*
> *Make beautiful my words,*
> *It is done in beauty*

Prologue

It is done in beauty
It is done in beauty
It is done in beauty.

He also shared intimate parts of his life with Eudora, such as the death of his daughter, Linda. He knew Eudora had "suffered grievous losses in recent years."[10]

The *New York Times Book Review* asked Eudora to review Ken's newest novel, *The Underground Man*. In January 1971, Eudora mailed her review to Ken for his "review." She asked if he objected to any of her observations. He didn't.[11] The *New York Times Book Review* published the review on Valentine's Day 1971, the one day a year set aside for sweethearts and lovers. Some later wondered if this was coincidence.[12]

In part, Eudora's review read:

> *What gives me special satisfaction about this novel, is that no one but a good writer—this good writer—could have possibly brought it off. It is not only exhilaratingly well done; it is also very moving…Mr. Macdonald's writing is something like a stand of clean, cool, well-branched trees in which bright birds can flash and perch. And not for show, but to sing.*[13]

Whether by fate or coincidence, Ken learned from friends that Eudora was staying at the same hotel as he, the Algonquin in New York. The afternoon of May 17, he waited in the lobby, hoping to see her. She entered the hotel. He watched her make her way to the desk to retrieve her room key. He had just received a letter from her in April. In it, Eudora had expressed her dislike for Arthur Mizener's biography of Ford Madox Ford, who had helped her and so many young writers. Ken immediately wrote Eudora back:

> *When I got your letter today, something went through me like a vibration of light, as if a responsive echo from a distant star. As if a half-imagined relationship to the great past had come real in my life before my life ended. It came down to me through you, through your defense of the tradition of humane letters…*

Prologue

Eudora responded:

> *I feel glad that I ever happened along when I did and the way I did, to be part of it—glad for my own sake, my own beliefs, too—I believe it was bound to happen for you somehow—But thank you for telling this, which has made me a part of some perfect occurrence—Nothing ever gave me that feeling before, and I doubt if anything ever will again.*

Before they met, they had heard each other's voices through their written words. They learned of each other's opinions, likes and dislikes. They sensed each other's strengths, weaknesses and sensitivities.

Now, here was Eudora standing before him. The sight of her tall, lean figure surely appeared much like a mirage. As Eudora made her way to the elevator, she heard from across the lobby, "Miss Welty? Kenneth Millar."

Unable to suppress her surprise, Eudora followed Ken back into the lobby. She threw her coat down and sat with him. Their conversation overflowed into the evening. When they were ready to retire, they discovered their rooms were adjacent.

Coincidence? Ken Millar did not believe in coincidences.

During their stay, Ken took Eudora to a cocktail party given by publishers Alfred and Helen Knopf in his honor. Then he took her to dinner. Eudora showed him the New York she had fallen in love with as a young girl—Manhattan and Broadway. As she did, Ken erupted to life, all eyes and ears, even when a cop ran past, gun pulled, chasing a man. They returned to the hotel after midnight. Before Ken left for his home in Canada, he left Eudora a message that read:

> *Dear Eudora: I never thought I'd hate to leave New York, but I do. I feel an unaccustomed sorrow not to be able to continue our friendship vive voce and in the flesh, but these are the chances of life. But there is a deeper and happier chance, which will keep us friends till death, don't you believe? And we'll walk and talk again. Til then, Ken. Meanwhile, there are letters.*

Prologue

During Eudora's stay at the Algonquin, she received from Ken a postcard that showed a picture of the Kissing Bridge in West Montrose, Ontario. On it, he wrote, "Treasuring fond memories of New York and you."[14] The two quickly fell in love[15] and began a long-distance relationship through letters. Ken never divorced his wife, but his and Eudora's love and admiration for each other remained buried between the lines they penned.

Eudora's longtime agent, Diarmuid Russell, and his wife, Rosie, would also attend the festivities, despite Diarmuid's poor health. Eudora immediately wrote to Ken to tell him the news:

> *Such a wonderful thing also happened in that Diarmuid Russell, who is ailing and frail, has decided he is going to come. He and his wife Rose, for all the times I've visited them, have never been here to see me. I'm terribly moved. They will of course be staying with me, and this means I am not asking other guests to stay at the house too—so although I did want you and Margaret to stay here if you could and would, I feel it's better all around just to have it this way, don't you?*[16]

On October 3, 1972, Diarmuid, wrote to Eudora with heartbreaking news:

> *Hate to tell you I got not very good news from my doctor—lung cancer and I go into the hospital this Thursday for some tests Friday, am told I may be let home for the weekend and then go back to have the operation on Wednesday. Dunno how long I will be out of action...I feel surprisingly philosophic about it all and only sorry that Rosie and friends have to worry too.*[17]

After his surgery, he began taking cobalt treatments and announced his retirement not long after.

Russell knew he needed to retire after he returned to work in January 1973. In March, he wrote to Eudora that Timothy Seldes, who had taken over the agency, would faithfully look after her.[18]

Eudora turned sixty-four on April 13, 1973, and still lived in her family home at 1117 Pinehurst Street. Passersby often saw her

Prologue

peering out her upstairs-bedroom window. Six years after her father built the home, his funeral was held there in September 1931.

Preparing for the festival and Eudora's special day, thoughts of her mother, father and two brothers must have crossed her mind and touched her heart often. As a renowned, award-winning author, she traveled extensively across the world, from New York to San Francisco, Mexico, Europe, England and Ireland. Even so, Eudora Welty was still simply Eudora. She often remembered how, after their family summer vacation, her father went through their closed-up, waiting house restarting all the clocks.[19]

> *The memory is a living thing—it, too, is in transit. But during its moment, all that is remembered joins and lives—the old and young, the past and the present, the living and the dead.*[20]

Chapter 1
Chessie and Chris
Leaving the Past

Newlyweds Christian Webb and Chestina Andrews Welty were packed and ready to leave. Among their suitcases and trunks were cherished personal items. There were letters Christian wrote to Chestina while he was away looking for their new home. There were treasured books neither could leave behind. The set of Charles Dickens belonged to Chestina. One book, entitled *Sanford and Merton*, held together by strips of pasted paper, had lost its cover. Another was a small keepsake book, and on one page was written: "April 15, 1886 My dearest Webbie: I want you to be a good boy and to meet me in heaven. Your loving Mother." These books belonged to Christian. There were also photograph negatives dated August 1903 of Thousand Falls, the place Chessie had not chosen as their new home.

They were leaving from Chestina's West Virginia home in Clay County, near Charleston. Years earlier, Chestina's father, Edward Raboteau "Ned" Andrews, had carefully selected the mountaintop site near the Elk River. He built their low wooden house with a wide hall down the middle, where sunlight gathered throughout the day.[21] Here his children were born and reared. Here his five sons' musical instruments reverberated through the walls. Here, long after his death, his grandchildren would visit. Family stories of the

Andrewses' wild, lonely mountainside were told and passed down many times.[22]

Coming from a long line of educators and preachers, Ned inherited a zeal for life. While attending Trinity College, he organized a literary society. He was a journalist and photographer. After settling in West Virginia, he became a lawyer and the county's youngest member of the bar. He had a gift for words, confidently arguing his cases and addressing his audience with literary finesse.[23] As daring as he was well spoken, the locals depended on him during emergencies. He took care of a threatening swarm of bees. He saved someone who had fallen into a deep well. Ned also hunted and fished with heroic flair, and years later, people still spoke of his feats. Ned Andrews could do anything—and did! His sense of humor flavored the tall tales he told his wife, Eudora Carden. He enjoyed playing harmless tricks on her with the assistance of a son or two. Eudora was named after her mother, Eudora Ayres. She came from a well-to-do planter family. When she married Virginian

Chessie and Chris: Leaving the Past

William Carden, her dowry of five slaves traveled with them to their mountain home. William was poor but brought with him a Latin dictionary. After reaching their destination, they set the slaves free but held on to William's dictionary. They kept it in their little farmhouse all those years.

Chestina was Ned and Eudora Andrews's first child. They called her Chessie. She was born to hold objects naturally in her left hand. Her father wanted her to be right-handed because the world was designed for right-handed people. He insisted that Chessie become right-handed. She did, but she also began to stutter.[24] Yet Ned's love and devotion for Chessie was evident. Once he so worried that her long hair would sap her strength that he asked her to cut it. Chessie stubbornly refused. Some fathers might have demanded their daughters cut their hair whether they liked it or not. Not Ned Andrews. He coaxed his daughter. He first offered to buy her a set of gold earrings if she allowed the scissors to touch her hair. She refused again.

Ned weighed his options and carefully selected the next deal to offer his daughter. Understanding her love for literature, he asked, "What about books? I'll have them send a whole set of Charles Dickens to you, right up the river from Baltimore, in a barrel."

This time, Chessie sacrificed her locks for the promised Dickens set. Her father promptly fulfilled that promise. Many nights in the quiet stillness, she hid beneath her bed reading Dickens in dim candlelight.[25]

As Chessie packed up the Charles Dickens set for travel, a gush of memories like this one must have stirred her more than once. She was only fifteen when her father became deathly ill. In agony, he lay on a quilted bed in the front room of the house. From there, he asked Chessie to bring him a kitchen knife and plunge it into his side, where the pain pounded. In shock, she wondered if she should obey him. His condition worsened. The family knew Ned needed help from a doctor. However, the snowy winter made the mountain roads impassible.

Leaving her mother to tend the boys, Chessie and her ailing father set out in the brutal cold night to find the nearest doctor. A neighbor came to their aid, offering his raft to float them across the Elk River.

The Inspiring Life of Eudora Welty

Icy winds swept over soaked clothing and bit through gloves, hats and coats. In these miserable conditions, Ned lay in pain by the fire they built in the middle of the raft. Chessie sat at his side. The neighbor poled through the ice, down and across the river. Once they made it to the railroad tracks, they waited for a train to flag down to take them to Baltimore.

At John Hopkins Hospital, Ned Andrews died from a ruptured appendix on the operating table. Steeped in grief, Chessie returned to her mountain home with her father's coffin and the weight of his death on her shoulders. She never forgot his last words to her: "If you let them tie me down, I'll die."

Ned Andrews's admiration for his wife lived on in his photos. In one, Eudora is dressed in her fine clothes. Her long, dark hair pulled high off her oval face has a flower tucked into the tresses. Her full lips are a dainty image beneath her strong cheekbones. Sitting slightly turned, her hands are crossed on the back of the chair, one over the other. The hands in this photo contrasted greatly to the hands

Chessie and Chris: Leaving the Past

Chessie saw daily. They were working hands that bled on frosty mornings after Eudora broke the ice on the well to retrieve water.

With the financial strain of a fatherless home, Eudora Carden Andrews depended on Chessie in many ways. To help make ends meet, Chessie became a teacher. Each day, she twirled her hair up into a bun. She mounted her horse and pulled her little brother up behind her. Through the countryside, they rode to the river, where she took a raft across. Her brother took the horse back home and returned for Chessie in the afternoon. In a one-room schoolhouse, Chessie taught students of all ages, some older than she was. The fathers came with the children to school to see if Chessie could handle their children. The fathers also wanted to see if she would stand up to them.

Chessie explained, "I'll have to whip the children if they refuse to go for water or set the school on fire. And if you care to contest this, then I'll be glad to give you a whipping, too." She quickly gained the respect of the parents. Though circumstances forced her to grow up swiftly, she paid her way through the nearby Marshall College.

For Christian Welty, it must have been difficult taking Chessie away from the mother who needed her and the brothers who idolized her. Being from Ohio made Christian somewhat of a foreigner to Chessie's family. After all, he was a Yankee. From the day he first met the five Andrews brothers, Chris remained "Mr. Welty" to them.

Chessie recognized the differences between her late father and her husband, whom she called Chris. Ned was a teaser and taleteller and rambunctious in song. Chris, however, was self-contained, reserved, patient and stable, always intent on the future. Yet there was at least one similarity. Both men photographed special moments of their loved ones. In the same way Ned Andrews had photographed his wife, Chris Welty photographed Chessie during their courtship, when he worked at a lumber company nearby.

The courting of Chessie Andrews was a simple pleasure in glorious mountaintop scenery. They went on long strolls up and down the railroad tracks. They stopped along the way to rest and chat. Chessie often brought with her a book to read during their stops. Chris would have his camera to record moments of their time together. They took turns taking photos of each other.

The Inspiring Life of Eudora Welty

During their engagement, Chris went down to Mississippi to explore the town where they would live. They missed each other terribly. If money allowed, Chris traveled thousands of miles to be with Chessie, if only for a few days. When travel was not possible, their letters, sometimes written twice a day, spoke what their lips could not.

No one understood why Chessie wanted to move to the swamps of Mississippi. Friends and family cautioned her about contracting malaria or even dying.[26] On Chris and Chessie's wedding day, rather than gaiety and congratulations after their vows, Chessie's young brother Moses dashed outside and threw himself on the ground. He sobbed.

Chris's and Chessie's upbringings had been very different. The Andrewses were town folk, most educated with professions outside the home. The Weltys were rural farmers near the town of Logan in Hocking County, Ohio. Their white, two-story farmhouse peeked through an apple orchard. Behind the house stood a large barn, as well as a grazing pasture and fields of corn and wheat that ran through rolling hills.

Chris's father, Jefferson Welty, had been the youngest of thirteen children. He and his wife, Allie, had named Chris after Jefferson's father, also named Christian Welty.[27] Chris's father chose farming as his lifetime trade. Chris Welty was choosing another life far away from Hocking County, Ohio.

After tearful goodbyes, Chessie left her Andrews family and her mountain home as a Welty. She and Chris traveled to the station to catch the train for St. Louis. Their honeymoon destination was the World's Fair and Louisiana Purchase Centennial Exposition. It had opened in 1904—a year late.

The sign read, "Man's Greatest Achievement, St. Louis World's Fair, Don't Fail to See It." The St. Louis World's Fair commemorated the centennial of the first important expansion in the United States. It also celebrated the purchase of the Louisiana Territory from France. Five miles from the Mississippi River in the western part of St. Louis, Missouri, the site spread over approximately 1,263 acres. Work on the site began in December 1901, when the land was primarily rolling hills and thick forest. The Des Peres, a slow but perilous river, flowed through. Maples and elms replaced the

Chessie and Chris: Leaving the Past

old virgin oaks cut to prepare the land. The St. Louis exposition exceeded previous expos. These were the Centennial at Philadelphia in 1876 (236 acres), the Chicago Exposition in 1893 (633 acres), Paris in 1900 (336 acres) and the Pan American in Buffalo in 1901 (300 acres). The St. Louis exposition consisted of more than one thousand buildings. Some were service buildings, like the powerhouse, garbage plant, pump rooms and hospital. Others were exhibit structures, such as the Mining Gulch, Model Street, the Indian School and the Anthropology Building.

The Inspiring Life of Eudora Welty

Christian and Chessie's day could have begun as early as 8:00 a.m., when the exposition gates opened. Day sights at the fair lasted until sunset, when all the exhibits, except the Palace of Art, closed. Visitors went to the Pike for concessions and amusements. They ambled along the walks of an Alpine Village. Switching on thousands of lights, the night scenes began and lasted until 11:30 p.m.

Divided into fifteen categories were seventy thousand exhibitors. Through investigation, the newlyweds would have encountered gardens, sculptures, watercourses and landscape designs typical to every foreign culture and climate. There were concerts, music competitions and other social activities, including athletic games, air-ship contests and military drills.

When their time at the fair ended, they left their pasts behind as best they could. With them, they took memories from the exposition. They headed for the place Chessie had chosen for their home.[28]

Chapter 2

Jackson, Mississippi

Forging Ahead

By 1908, Chris and Chessie Welty had settled in Jackson, Mississippi. Jackson still struggled to find its way out of Reconstruction, to find progress and to earn its place as the capital of Mississippi. The war had wounded the entire population, both black and white. These wounds had never been treated, much less healed.

Only forty-five years earlier, on May 14, 1863, Union troops had occupied Mississippi's capital city during the War Between the States. General Ulysses S. Grant and General William Tecumseh Sherman were already there when the Union troops marched into Jackson. They came by way of the Mississippi Springs Road (Raymond Road). McPherson's Fifty-ninth Indiana Infantry, First Brigade, Seventh Division, XVII Corps, entered via the Clinton Road (West Capitol). The Fifty-ninth Indiana Infantry raised its colors over the capitol.

Sherman had one day to destroy Jackson, the state's manufacturing and transportation center. Grant ordered that destruction be limited to only facilities and supplies supporting the Confederate war effort. Union forces burned foundries, arsenals, cotton mills and bridges and pulled up railroad tracks. When Sherman learned that his Union soldiers had pillaged the stores, he warned the brigade commander, Brigadier General Joseph A. Mower, to "take only what is necessary. The feeling of pillage and booty will injure the morals of the troops and bring disgrace to our cause." Even so, troops burned churches, hotels, stores, hospitals and private residences. Sherman blamed the burning of the penitentiary on the convicts. He also blamed the excessive damage and ruin on "camp-followers" and the "effect of some bad rum." He admitted the devastation "was not justified by the rules of war." Still, the Union troops escaped disciplinary measures.

For whatever reason, the torch missed the capitol, the Governor's Mansion and city hall. Also spared was the Manship House, built in 1857. The owner, Charles Henry Manship, who had served as alderman and postmaster, was mayor of Jackson. He surrendered the city of Jackson to General Sherman on July 6, 1864.

After the war, under the Constitution of 1868, newly elected governor James Lusk Alcorn and his administration had the job of repairing the damage. They also were to renovate the capitol and the Governor's Mansion. Serious contemplation and conversations within the legislature had some representatives determined to move the capitol from Jackson. After all, the town had never thrived or grown. Commerce relied mainly on river and railroad transportation. The cities of Meridian and Vicksburg overshadowed Jackson in both commerce and population. Vicksburg leaders asked the legislature to move the capitol to their city. There were discussions of moving it to Kosciusko. The discussions died after the Mississippi legislature appropriated $70,000 to repair the state capitol and the Governor's Mansion.[29]

For Mississippi, Reconstruction ended in 1875. In 1890, specially elected delegates to a constitutional convention gathered at the Old Capitol. Debates included literacy tests and poll taxes as requirements for voting. The tests would keep almost all black voters from the polls. The poll tax would keep large numbers of blacks and whites from voting. This new constitution was not sent to the people for ratification.

In 1896, the United States Supreme Court decision in *Plessy v. Ferguson* ruled that states could require separate but equal facilities for blacks and whites. Two years later, in *Williams v. Mississippi*, the court upheld provisions of the 1890 constitution, denying African

JACKSON, MISSISSIPPI: FORGING AHEAD

Americans certain civil rights—particularly their voting rights. Mississippi's new state flag demonstrated the desire to cling to the past. Adopted in 1894, the new flag contained the Confederate battle flag. By 1900, the state's population was composed of 59 percent African Americans. Passed in 1908, the Grandfather Clause to the new constitution permitted some illiterate whites to vote but prevented most African Americans from doing so. Using both legal and illegal means, white officials controlled and intimidated black citizens. One of the most barbaric means of controlling was lynching. Lynching was the unlawful hanging or killing of a person by mob action. In the nineteenth and twentieth centuries, the lynching of African Americans in the South was commonplace to maintain white supremacy. These appalling measures would haunt Mississippi for years to come.[30]

By 1900, the Old Capitol and the Governor's Mansion were in grave disrepair. In 1902, legislators created the Mississippi Department of Archives and History to collect, care for and preserve old records. Dunbar Rowland, a thirty-seven-year-old attorney from Coffeeville, headed the new agency. After his inspection of the premises, Rowland exposed the deplorable conditions of the Old Capitol. Neglect of important documents and records had lasted over three decades. To help remedy this problem, in 1906 the Mississippi legislature leased the Old Capitol to the Mississippi Industrial Exposition Company for holding a state fair. Although it paid only ten dollars annually, it was to be responsible for keeping the windows and roof in good repair. In addition, it was to remove all sheds, booths, signs and other obstructions between the building and State Street. Another obligation was to protect and preserve all books, records and archives in the building that were not transferred to Rowland's location in the new capitol.

The exposition company failed to hold up its end of the contract. Dunbar advised Mississippi governor James K. Vardaman of the ghastly conditions of state records. Since 1904, bills to restore the Old Capitol had never made it past the committee. Discussions of demolishing the Old Capitol and selling the grounds resumed.

In the new capitol, with its gleaming dome, legislators gathered for their first session in 1904. Taxes owed by the railroad companies to the State of Mississippi helped fund the construction of the new capitol. The state fair opened in late October or early November. Flags and banners decorated the exterior of the Old Capitol, which held the gated entrance to the fair. Exhibits were in some of the rooms. Entertainment was on the grounds. Visitors walked through the gate, around the capitol and to the back steps leading down to the fairgrounds. Memories of the World's Fair in St. Louis and their passion for learning and entertainment surely had Chris and Chessie joining the crowds at the fairgrounds.

The new era of steam locomotives began to supersede steamboats. Inland towns outgrew river towns. Closing out the nineteenth century, Vicksburg and Meridian remained the larger towns, with populations of more than fourteen thousand. Jackson's population had reached seven thousand, but the city was rapidly growing. Electric streetcars replaced mule-driven carts. Clanging bells warned pedestrians of their approach. The main shopping district in Jackson was on Capitol Street. The Old Capitol stood as its crown. Businesses flocked to the district. Many joined an exodus from South State Street, like Kennington's Department Store and Batte Furniture Store, one of the oldest businesses in Jackson. Capital National Bank stood at the corner of Capitol and West Streets, not far from the *Clarion-Ledger* offices, Jackson's daily newspaper. On special occasions, the Weltys likely dined at Bon Ton Café, Jackson's finest restaurant on West Capitol Street.

Churches of every denomination sprang up on corners. Temple Beth Israel was on South State and South Streets. First Methodist Church was on the corner of Yazoo and Congress Streets. During the Civil War, First Methodist served as a Confederate hospital and a base for hospital supplies. It was burned by Sherman's troops. The Weltys would later become members of the new church, which was renamed Galloway Methodist Church.

After the war, freed African Americans lived in separate and unequal environments. They were restricted in terms of where they could do business. They built flourishing businesses and residential districts that included Farish, Amite, Fortification, Mill and Lamar Streets. Many attended Pearlie Grove Missionary Baptist Church on South Farish Street.

Jackson, Mississippi: Forging Ahead

Chartered in February 1906 with a capital stock of $50,000, the Lamar Mutual Life Insurance Company began operations on April 6, 1906. It was located in a suite of three rented offices in the Medical Building on Capitol Street in Jackson, next to the Century Theatre. A.C. Jones was the first president of the company. Christian Welty was the cashier. Sometime during 1906, Lamar Mutual purchased as its home office the two-story building next to the Pythian Castle on Capitol Street. True to the term "castle," the Pythian resembled a historic castle. From its roof waved an American flag.[31]

Jackson, Mississippi, was Chris and Chessie's home now, far away from West Virginia and Ohio. Much like the town they lived in, along with success, they faced hardships. In their first residence, a fire had broken out. Central Fire Station, the first paid fire department in Jackson, probably sent its horse-drawn, hook-and-ladder wagon. Chestina and Christian escaped the fire without harm. Though Chessie was still recovering from a recent illness, she could not bear the thought of flames consuming her volumes of Dickens. She hobbled on crutches back into the blazing building to save her books. From an open window, she tossed each volume onto the lawn before getting herself back to safety. Imagine her standing close to her scattered books, beside her husband, sweating from the heat, coughing from the smoke. The books, wet and charred, were safe again in their new home on North Congress Street. So were Christian's two childhood books, nestled among the others on the shelves. The damaged leather of Chessie's books would remind her of this day forever. How often would they remind her that some things can be saved while other things cannot?

The birth of a first child is a glorious occasion. In 1905, before the fire, Chestina and Christian had welcomed their firstborn, a son. They named him Christian. Friends and business colleagues in Jackson would have dropped by the Welty home to welcome the new addition and left calling cards if mother and baby were resting. Congratulatory flowers on tables and mantels scented the room. As Christian grew, there would have been gleeful moments over his first tooth. Both Chessie and Chris would have coaxed him into his first crawl. Their watchful eyes and protective hands would have kept young Christian from sharp objects, stairways and open doors and

placed breakable items out of his reach. When her son grew tired and sleepy, like any new mother, Chestina surely pulled him into her lap to sing or read him to sleep.

Young Christian was a little over a year old when both he and Chestina became ill. The doctor gave Chestina little hope for survival. Septicemia had set in, and she was unable to eat. In those days, few survived septicemia, a life-threatening infection that worsened quickly. So serious was the illness that they cut off Chestina's long hair. Christian took the locks, placed them in a bag

Jackson, Mississippi: Forging Ahead

and put the bag away. Though the doctors held little hope, Chris would not surrender his wife to death. If only he could find food she could keep down—maybe then she could regain her strength.

Medicinally, champagne was used to treat several ailments, including nausea and vomiting. Christian Welty turned to this remedy, even though wine was not allowed in Jackson.

In Canton, Mississippi, there lived an Italian orchard grower named Mr. Trolio. Christian called and asked Mr. Trolio to put a bottle of his wine on the Number 3 train, which would be stopping at the Canton station to take on water before chugging its way into Jackson. Mr. Trolio quickly chose a bottle, buried it in a bucket of ice and placed it on the Number 3. When the train arrived, Christian snatched it from the baggage car. He rushed to Chestina's bedside and offered her a glass of chilled champagne. The champagne settled her stomach. Chestina was able to eat again. Slowly, she regained her strength. Young Christian did not. He died in 1907 at the age of fifteen months. The question "Why did I live and not him?" haunted Chestina. Just like the young girl who years earlier had carried on after the death of her father, so Chestina carried on after the death of her firstborn child.

Baby Christian was buried in the cemetery just down the street, within sight of the house. After the services, Chestina removed the two polished buffalo nickels that lay on Christian's eyes. She placed them on cotton inside a small, white cardboard box. In the same bureau that held the long switch of hair Chris had saved, she placed the box that housed the nickels, the only keepsake of her oldest child. There were no photos of Baby Christian, but had there been? After all, Chris was an avid photographer. Seeing to her treatment had caused everyone to forget about the baby, Chessie thought. Her son died. She lived, and her hair grew back long.[32]

Chapter 3
Early Childhood

Imagination

In the Deep South, April turns the ground into the deepest greens. Scents of the chinaberry flower, rose, jasmine, daylily, iris and honeysuckle ride the breezes.³³ Spring brings forth new life in Mississippi. Spring also delivered new life to the Welty home: a baby girl born on April 13, 1909. The first first-generation Mississippian in their family, they named her Eudora Alice Welty. She was named for her Andrews grandmother, Eudora Carden, and her Welty grandmother, Chris's mother, who died when he was a boy. She was called Allie. Chris assumed this was short for Alice. Not until after Eudora's christening did he learn his mother's name was Almira. Even so, Eudora retained her middle name: Alice.

Evening strolls were customary this time of year. Lightning bugs flashed in and out of the hydrangea waiting for its buds and the azaleas in full bloom. Residents gathered on sidewalks to catch up with the latest news and gossip while their children ran and played. One topic on North Congress Street was probably the Weltys. Once again, a baby's cry filled the Welty house. Those nearby who knew of their loss a few years back might have paused to offer up a prayer of thanksgiving or speak of their good fortune. On the night of Haley's comet, those who happened to glance over at 741 North Congress Street would have seen Chris Welty at the window. He held his sleeping infant daughter and pointed to the fiery tail in the sky.[34]

Into an album, Chessie arranged the many pictures Chris took of Eudora with his folding Kodak. Underneath each photo, she placed a caption. One was of Chessie on their front porch in her fine black hat looking down at baby Eudora in her christening gown. There was one of Eudora wearing her new bonnet and one of a family trip to Ohio and West Virginia after Eudora's birth. Another showed Eudora attempting her first steps. Eudora became the center of Chris and Chessie's world.[35] Baby Christian became a silent memory.

On the backdoor steps of their house, a very young Eudora sat. The family chickens pecked the feed scattered around her. Birds were her best friends and playmates. She sometimes pulled one onto her lap and held it like a baby. When Easter fell close to Eudora's birthday, Chessie decorated the tables with bunny rabbit favors. She pulled Eudora's hair back with a large ribbon to match her best Sunday dress. On the front steps, Eudora curled one leg up under her and waited. Her dainty parasol lay open on the step above her. Once her guests arrived, they played games like "Frog in the Middle" on the lawn.[36]

Eudora had easy access to every room, every book and every instrument. Her curiosity, intense observations and need to know details had Eudora searching for Chessie throughout the house, book in hand. Once Eudora found her, she handed the book to her mother. Chessie understood the importance of reading and the power of the written word. She surrendered to Eudora's yearning for story after story. As Chessie relaxed by a sizzling coal fire or churned in the kitchen, she read to Eudora. Coming from a long line of storytellers, Chessie recited dramatically so Eudora experienced the characters and the settings in which their creator placed them.[37]

Eudora received her parents' undivided attention until her brother Edward Jefferson Welty was born in 1912. Walter Andrews Welty was born three years later. He was calmer and more serious than his older siblings. Still, they included him in their fun and made plays in which Eudora was the producer and director, as well as entertainer. Edward and Eudora seemed kindred spirits. They delighted in each other's comedy. Eudora's imagination came as

EARLY CHILDHOOD: IMAGINATION

easy as her humor. Her keen sense of humor developed early and came naturally. It had likely filtered down from the Andrews side of the family. Edward played off both with his own antics. On the floor, book open, Eudora read to Edward "The Four Little Children Who Went Around the World." Each time Eudora came to the names of the children, she and Edward gleefully shouted together, "Violet, Slingsby, Guy and Lionel!" Something about these names made them fall into uncontrollable fits of laughter. Laughing fits like this sometimes accompanied them to the dinner table, a time reserved for calm reflections of the day. Once Eudora and Edward got started laughing, they couldn't stop. Their dinners grew cold. Frustrated and still somewhat amused, Chessie finally ordered them to leave the table.[38]

Laughter is indeed a medicine. Even when Eudora and her brothers lay sick in their upstairs beds, laughter seeped through their closed bedroom doors. To pass the time, they drew pictures and wrote notes to one another. Chessie sterilized the notes in a hot oven before delivering them, curled up and a little scorched, to

the recipients. During the Spanish influenza epidemic, Edward and Eudora lay feverish in their beds. Eudora wrote to Edward: "There was a little boy and his name was Lindsey. He went to heaven with the influenzy."

Lindsey, a boy in their neighborhood, was also bedridden with influenza. Eudora heard her father and mother whispering about him. "I wonder how poor little Lindsey got along today," one would say. Chestina read this jingle before placing it inside the oven. She was horrified her daughter had turned a child's sickness into lighthearted verse that ended in death. Certainly, Eudora meant no harm, but Chessie did not tolerate such disregard for life. She refused to deliver the note. Chris scolded Eudora and told her it was not funny.

"You ought to be ashamed of yourself," Chestina cried. "And if you can't be ashamed of yourself, then I'll have to be ashamed for you."[39]

Chris and Chessie stood firm together on this situation. On occasion, however, they contradicted each other. During thunderstorms, Chris swiftly pulled the children away from the windows. Always the protector, he prepared for the worst. He even scored the bottoms of Eudora's new shoes with his silver pocketknife so she wouldn't slip on a polished floor. Chessie, too, sheltered her children with every breath. But when it came to storms, she felt fear was unwarranted.

"High winds never bothered me in West Virginia," she said. "Just listen at that. I wasn't a bit afraid of a little lightning and thunder. I'd go out on the mountain, spread my arms wide, and run in a good big storm."[40] Unafraid, Chessie stood at the window away from which her husband had pulled the children and watched the driving rain and lightning slice into dark, sinister clouds. She must have seemed brave and daring to all her children.

Chris Welty satisfied his children's curiosity with books. The Lincoln Library of Information, a set of Stoddard lectures and the Victrola Book of the Opera lined the shelves in the living room, also known as the library. Books were thumbed through, read and studied. The large dictionary on the wooden stand remained opened to the last word looked up.

Chris preferred nonfiction books. They held truth. The contents were dependable, solid. Nonfiction provided a greater sense of the

Early Childhood: Imagination

world. He once told Eudora, "If you're ever lost in a strange country, look for where the sky is brightest along the horizon. That reflects the nearest river. Strike out for a river and you will find habitation."[41]

Chessie never cared for embellished stories—gossip, she called it. She made it a point to tend to her family business, not someone else's. On the other hand, she preferred fiction, like *Jane Eyre* and *Green Mansions*, grand stories about people and relationships. She wanted external conflicts, internal struggles. She liked characters, plots and settings in dramas that pulled you into the pages. Consequently, Eudora had at her disposal both fiction and nonfiction. Her favorites were the *Book of Knowledge*, *Our Wonder World*, a set of Mark Twain and Ring Lardner's writing. These Eudora pulled off the shelves and down to the floor. Within the pages, she appreciated the real and unreal. She learned how to know truth by recognizing a lie.[42]

Through her father's passion for instruments, Eudora learned by doing. On breezy days, her family drove out of the city into the country. Fields rolled into the horizon, and cattle and horses grazed on tall grasses. Chris found the perfect clear spot to fly the box kite he made. Out in a grassy opening, Chessie operated the spindle of cord, and Chris ran with the kite until it caught wind. They watched it take flight. Chessie then handed the spindle to Eudora, Edward or Walter to feel the pull of the wind.

On Christmas mornings, Eudora ran downstairs knowing there would be books waiting for her. The aroma of homemade fruitcake lingered in the toasty air. When she was younger, her new baby dolls became as real to her as her brothers. Eudora led them through scenes that she conjured up. Later, her paper dolls became actors in the scripts she wrote for the tiny theater she directed. Still later, she found a princess bike under the tree. Outside, she rode with other neighborhood children. Some glided alongside in new skates.

To Chris, tinker toys, rector sets and other play items that required assembly made the perfect Christmas gifts. They required thinking and design. Edward and Walter carried their new train set upstairs. After assembly, they enjoyed the sight of the train winding around the curves, its headlight beaming through tunnels and across the bridges. For hours, the train ran into the night. Downstairs, Eudora listened to its perpetual whine, traveling round and round.[43]

The Inspiring Life of Eudora Welty

Like her mother, Eudora had been born left-handed. Like her grandfather, Chris knew the world was designed for right-handed people. Just as Chessie's father had made Chessie use her right hand, Chris made Eudora use hers. Left-handers ran in the Andrews family. Chessie's five brothers were lefties. Chessie had been a lefty. Ned Andrews had been ambidextrous. Chessie told Chris she feared that by forcing Eudora to be right-handed, she would stutter, too. At times, Chessie still stumbled over her words. Even so, Eudora learned to use her right hand.

Beneath a blackboard sky on which was drawn the moon and thousands of stars, Chris set up his telescope in the front yard. With one hand, he positioned Eudora at the scope. His other hand adjusted the focus. Chris brought the moon down to Eudora. Planets revolve around the sun. Earth's moon revolves around the Earth, changing shape according to its alignment with the sun. All this Eudora learned at their library table, along with the names of constellations and the myths connected to them.[44]

Stored in a black buckram box was Chris's kaleidoscope and gyroscope, which he set dancing on a string. He explained the function of each instrument. The kaleidoscope uses a prism of mirrors to generate symmetric patterns of light and color from asymmetric objects. Chris challenged his children with puzzles composed of metal rings and intersecting links and keys chained together. The movement of each puzzle he demonstrated slowly, patiently. He handed the puzzle over to each of his children to be tried repeatedly, without success.

The sun lay low in the horizon. After supper, neighborhood children slipped back outside with little steamboats they made out of shoeboxes. Windows were cut out in the shape of the sun, moon and stars. Colored tissue paper covered the windows. A candle was lit inside. Up and down the sidewalk they ran, pretending to be steamboats on the Mississippi River. Eudora pulled her shoebox over the cracks in the sidewalk. She was careful not to bump and topple the candle. Not once did her box catch on fire. One Armistice Day, Eudora and her brothers made their own parade on a single velocipede. Edward peddled, Walter sat on the handlebars and Eudora stood on the back, arms wide, waving flags in both hands.

EARLY CHILDHOOD: IMAGINATION

Chris snapped a photograph of them passing by. On Eudora's street, there were always sand piles to dig in, trees to climb and lightning bugs to catch. Darkness crept in and swallowed the last morsel of light. Front doors opened, and mothers called their children home.[45]

Summer nights in Mississippi can be sweltering, and breezes rare. The screech of insects cuts into the thick humidity. Barking dogs in the distance sound lost and lonesome. Tucked in for the night on the sleeping porch, Eudora lay awake. The sounds turned night into a living, breathing creature. This was when she traveled backward, remembering the events of the day. The sounds of morning were her father whistling a song and her mother humming back the same tune. One was upstairs, the other downstairs. Back and forth their melody traveled to each other. It was a song Eudora knew: "The Merry Widow."[46] She might remember the old man carrying a croaker sack slung over his shoulder. The Welty servant told her the sack was for carrying off bad little children. Eudora didn't believe her. Yet, she wondered.[47] Some nights, Mr. and Mrs. Holt, who lived two houses down, entertained themselves and, unknowingly, their neighbors as well. Mrs. Holt banged the piano. Mr. Holt sang out in his high, robust voice, "Oho ye oho ye, who's bound for the ferry, the briar's in bud and the sun's going down." People were so different—in their manners and gestures, their speech and the way they dealt with life. This Eudora also pondered.[48]

At night, the ear searches for a familiar sound. It may be the person climbing the stairway. It could be the running water down the hall. Every night, Eudora listened to the tick-tock of her father's striking clocks. He loved timepieces. At midnight, the gong of the mission-style oak grandfather clock in the hall woke her. The striking clock in her parents' room answered. Then the cuckoo clock struck in the dining room. The kitchen clock, however, never uttered a sound. Time was always ticking, always moving forward.[49]

Chapter 4
World War I
Curiosity

Theodore Bilbo won the 1915 governor's race for the state of Mississippi. During his tenure, the legislature established the State Highway Commission in 1916. The same year, it passed the bill to renovate the Old Capitol as a state office building. Demolition of the interior began that summer. Regardless of his accomplishments as governor, Bilbo would become one the most controversial government officials in American history. He would help make Mississippi one of the most controversial states in the country.[50]

On April 2, 1917, just before Eudora's eighth birthday, President Woodrow Wilson called for the declaration of war against Germany. The year before, the First Mississippi Infantry had been called into service for the Mexican border action. The United States had not fought a major war in over fifty years. So, unprepared for war, the French and British had to sell ammunition, artillery and tanks to the American troops. The draft helped grow the military force needed, but every man and woman was ready to volunteer. About fifty-eight thousand Mississippians served in the United States military during the course of World War I.

Good-bye, Maw!
Good-bye, Paw!

The Inspiring Life of Eudora Welty

Good-bye, Mule!
With yer old hee-haw!
I'll git you a Turk
An' a Kaiser too-
An' that's about all
One feller can do![51]

In 1918, the Mississippi legislature ratified the Eighteenth Amendment to the United States Constitution. This amendment made selling alcohol illegal. In the same year, Mississippi became the last state to make it mandatory for children go to school.

Factories worked around the clock. Civilians organized war-bond rallies. The fruit pits they saved were burned to make charcoal filters for gas masks. The American government launched four drives to sell Liberty bonds. Celebrities and volunteer salespeople took war bond campaigns into neighborhoods across the United States. Women and children glued their twenty-five-cent stamps into Liberty Books— "Lick a Stamp and Lick the Kaiser" —raising $17 billion for the war effort. In Mississippi, the purchase of Liberty Loan bonds and war savings stamps produced more than $80 million. Women filled the jobs left behind by the men. They became mechanics, streetcar conductors, elevator operators and assembly line workers. The navy took on around eleven thousand women as yeomen. They did shore duty at the wireless stations and served as stenographers and clerks.

The Mississippi Cooperative Extension Service supervised home demonstration agents who organized local canning clubs and urged neighborhood victory gardens. Pledges like "One Can for the Government" were promised. Families refrained from eating certain foods on certain days of the week to conserve food for the army. People of all ages and races participated in American Red Cross chapters. They practiced first aid, prepared bandages and made clothing. They packed supplies into the boxes they assembled and sent them to American soldiers.[52]

Motorists observed gasless Sundays by hitching up teams of horses to the front bumpers of their vehicles and taking patriotic trips. On heatless Mondays, people conserved coal. Food administrator Herbert Hoover initiated wheatless Mondays and Wednesdays,

WORLD WAR I: CURIOSITY

meatless Tuesdays and porkless Thursdays and Saturdays. When preparing Eudora's school lunches, Chessie made sure they were wheatless and meatless on the required days. So did the other mothers in the neighborhood.

Looking down Capitol Street from the Old Capitol, the Jackson scene was still quite serene. Model-Ts filled downtown parking spaces. Horse-drawn wagons crossed at intersections. Baked goods were sold from a car with "McGough's Bread and Cake Factory" painted on the sides. Ten cents bought a standard loaf of bread.

Town Creek, which ran through downtown, often flooded in hard rains. In 1916, the creek reached flood level. It flowed through Capitol Street at Lamar and Farish Streets, flooding the F.W. Woolworth five-and-ten-cent store and the Majestic Cinema next door. During these floods, people gathered downtown. Men dressed in dark business suits and hats and women in long skirts, white blouses and the customary hat surveyed the flood damage.[53] Chris Welty was likely one of the crowd.

Lamar Mutual grew steadily under the leadership of its president, William Q. Cole. Chris continued to be a devoted employee. The company sold insurance in Tennessee and Alabama and grew modestly during World War I.[54]

Sounds of livestock, neighborly chatter and playing children breathed life into the surrounding residential neighborhoods. North Congress Street was still dirt and gravel. Little had changed for the Weltys except the sizes of their children's clothes and shoes.

Chessie was busy in the kitchen preparing her meal when she called out, "Quick! Who'd like to run to the little store for me?"

Eudora stopped what she was doing and hurried to her mother. "I would!"[55]

Placing money into Eudora's hand, Chessie explained what she needed from the little store. Eudora was nine now and could go to the store by herself. She began her route: a block down the street toward the capitol, then a half block farther and around the corner, in the direction of the cemetery.

On the way, Eudora observed everything. She soaked in the sounds and scenes where people carried through moments of their lives. Taking a journey alone lets you study the trivial and the spectacular.

The Inspiring Life of Eudora Welty

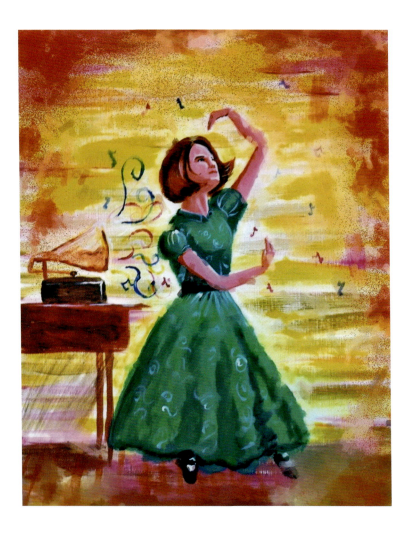

You can imagine. You can dream. You can build on what you see and wonder about what you don't see.

At one house along the way, three teenage sisters danced past a window. Their hair was piled high and pulled back in headbands. They sang, "Everybody ought to know-oh, how to do the tickle-toe, how to do the tickle-toe." Eudora knew this tune well.

Her mother always sang to them, lullabies that held a longing for something—"Wee Willie Winkies," "Bobby Shafftoe" and "Rock-a-Bye Baby." Eudora was allowed to wind up their Victrola and

World War I: Curiosity

play any record in the house. To songs like "When the Midnight Choo-Choo Leaves for Alabam" and "Kiss Me Again," she danced around the dining room much like the three sisters. Movement, Eudora thought, was the very heart of listening.[56]

Nearing the house across the street, Eudora slowed to a snail's crawl. This house scared her because it was where her principal, Miss Duling, lived. What if she peered out the window and saw Eudora walking by? What if she bolted out the door, onto her porch and shouted, "Eudora Alice Welty! Spell OBLIGE"?[57]

Just after Christmas, the year Eudora turned five, Chessie had marched her across the street to Jefferson Davis Grammar School. The newly built brick school was two stories high, with two big halls upstairs and down. A hedge grew along the front, and there were trees in the yard.

Chessie asked Miss Duling if she could register Eudora for first grade.

"Oh, all right. Probably the best thing you could do with her," Miss Duling said.

Miss Duling had big, half-moon eyebrows. Her black hair, severely pulled into a tight bun, made her nose look large. Dressed in her usual white gingham dress beneath a thick red wool sweater, her black stockings disappeared into black high-top shoes that pounded the floor. To Eudora, Miss Duling seemed supernatural and all-powerful. Yet she was beautiful, lively and spirited. Miss Duling was not married. The Jackson Public School System did not allow teachers to marry and have children of their own.

Miss Duling rang a big brass bell. *Clang! Clang!* For blocks, the school bell was heard at eight o'clock every weekday morning. Children walking from State, North and Jefferson Streets came to Davis School the back way. They plodded through the backyards, through other people's gardens. Chessie disliked how the children cut through the yards on North Congress Street. Some children rode their bicycles to school. Some rode horses. Boys wore short pants or rompers. They lined up at the south side of the school. Girls wore dresses. In winter, they added a union suit, stockings and lace-up, high-top shoes. An unexpected snow or ice brought worried mothers to school to deliver union suits. Their daughters donned them in the girls' basement restroom. Thankfully, Chessie was not one of these mothers, saving Eudora from embarrassment. The girls lined up on the north side. At the clang of Miss Duling's bell, everyone marched into the building together. The piano loudly played "Dorothy: An Old Country Dance." First through third graders marched to their classrooms on the first floor. Fourth through seventh graders marched upstairs to theirs.

Davis School had no electric lights since students attended only during the day. In summer, open windows beckoned breezes to join them in the classrooms. On rainy days, windows were closed. Rain slapped against the panes. Ominous clouds blocked the light. Darkness spilled into the classroom, excusing students from lessons they could not see. Eudora's teacher, Miss Louella Varnado, oversaw their spelling match in the dark. Down the hall, Miss McWillie, the teacher Eudora feared most, stood at the window. There, Miss McWillie gathered enough light to read stories like "King of the Golden River" to her students.

Clang! Clang! Time for little recess. Girls and boys lined up at the classroom door. They marched in their lines through the hallways and out the doors. In the yard, they separated. Boys went to the right and girls to the left. Eudora and her friends played jacks and jump-roped to chants like "Salt-pepper-vinegar-mustard-hot." The boys played ball or marbles.

Clang! Clang! This bell was for big recess and lunchtime. Students collected their lunch pails filled with delicious homemade sandwiches. Thermoses were filled with milk or, on cold days, hot chocolate. Again, they lined up in a perfectly straight line and headed out to the yard. Lunch was a highly anticipated event of the day. Long before the bell rang, classmates had passed notes that asked, "What do you have for lunch?" Those who brought lunches worthy of swapping received another note: "Let's eat lunch together." At lunch, also, boys and girls separated to opposite sides of the yard. Eudora's classmates swapped lunches with one another and ate beneath the shade tree. Out on the yard, Miss Duling sold half-pint milk bottles for a nickel. Another nickel bought a cream puff or other treats from the bread wagon. When it rained, students ate in the basement, which was freezing no matter what time of year.[58]

World War I: Curiosity

Sometimes the bell clanged at odd hours during the day, as was the case with the fire drill. About two thirty in the afternoon, Miss Duling rang her last bell. *Clang! Clang!* Students filed out of the building the same way they came in.

Miss Duling selected words to teach, direct and change one's mind. At times, she entered the classroom and told the teacher to sit down. Across the floor she went, heels clomping. At the chalkboard, she started her arithmetic lesson. She might call out a spelling test to see how the students were doing. One year, she sent the fourth grade students to the capitol. They competed in a spelling match against the legislators. The students won. Even Jackson's top politicians and leaders yielded to Miss Duling's direction. Rumors traveled throughout Jackson about Miss Duling's whipping machine in her office, hidden beneath a cover. No one, not one person, had ever seen it. No one wanted to.[59]

As strict as Miss Duling was to her students, the truth be told, Eudora could be quite a handful. At home, she argued and pouted when she didn't get her way. She pitched tantrums, slammed drawers and threw punches. She even packed her bags to leave home. One time, Eudora climbed high into a tree but couldn't get down. Below, Chris, Chessie, Edward and Walter watched Eudora scream and strike her head against the tree because no one climbed up to help her down. Chris said something like, "No one can get you down but you."

Chris and Chessie held high expectations for Eudora in school. Chessie searched the Jackson newspapers for Eudora's name listed among the honor roll students. Eudora dreaded exams. She was scared of not being able to meet her mother's expectations of a perfect score. Chris, though more understanding of a "less than perfect" grade, believed Eudora was above average, and her scores should reflect the same.

"Now, just keep remembering, the examinations were made out for the average student to pass," he explained to her. "That's the majority. And if the majority can pass, think how much better you can do."

This advice could have been confusing. After all, her father had required Eudora to give up her left-handedness to fit in with the majority.

THE INSPIRING LIFE OF EUDORA WELTY

When it came to academics, Eudora rarely disappointed her parents or teachers. Eudora craved knowledge like her father and mother. She excelled in school and enjoyed the honor roll free season tickets to the Jackson Senators baseball games. Classmate Nash Burger, also on the honor roll, was there, too.[60]

Without interference, Eudora passed by Miss Duling's house and continued her journey to the little store. The sidewalk faded away into old brick close to where the boy Lindsey lived. On this part of the sidewalk, roots of a chinaberry tree pushed through

World War I: Curiosity

the patterned brick walk. Eudora and her friends often skated down here. She knew to avoid fallen chinaberries that threatened smooth gliding and promised skinned knees. She knew at the bump in the bricks to take a quick hop over and try not to touch the ground.

Next to a row of houses with manicured yards stood a plain two-story brick building on a lot that had no yard, no trees and no flowerbeds—the little store. Eudora stepped from a sunny outside into the darker, cool interior of the store. Immediately, she smelled the dill-pickle brine, licorice and ammonia-loaded ice that cooled blocks of sweet butter. In the sunbeams penetrating the windows and open door, dust motes from crackers, flour and cornmeal flew about. The same dust covered floors and counters, though cloth and broom constantly labored for cleanliness.

In the back of the store a woman sat studying her ledger, pencil pinched between her fingers. The man who ran the store ambled about, waiting on customers. The two seemed old with their gray hair and round faces. Yet they were mysterious, their eyes hidden behind dark shades. Still, Eudora held no dread as she did at Miss Duling's house. She delighted in the marbles, wooden tops, bubble pipes and kite string. Most toys were defective in some way, like the rubber ball that didn't bounce straight. It didn't matter. This merchandise meant to entice children served its purpose well.

Eudora told the man what Chessie needed. He filled her order as she looked around. There was candy, lots of candy—Baby Ruths, Tootsie Rolls, Hershey bars, peppermints, suckers and gumdrops. She inched her way through the store, past the barrel of ice water where different kinds of pop were submerged like submarines. One was Eudora's favorite, the locally bottled Lake's Celery.

Eudora handed over the money and got her mother's order. The change was a shiny nickel she had permission to spend. This was the hardest part of the trip, figuring out what to buy with that nickel. Today, she chose Lake's Celery.

At the door, the man waited, as if he had read Eudora's mind. All the children wanted to weigh before leaving the little store. Eudora stopped at the standing scales, with its brass slide on the balance

The Inspiring Life of Eudora Welty

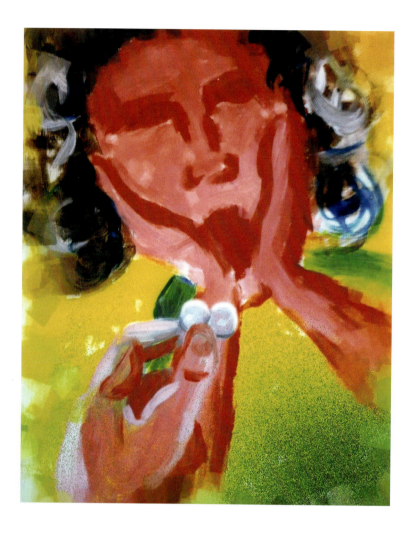

arm and a stack of iron weights. She handed him her bag to hold. He lifted Eudora up onto the scales, reminding her to stand real still so he could read her weight.

Eudora stepped out into the sunny day. Today, there were no brothers to call her a scare-cat. Sometimes, they dared her to take the other way home, through the storm sewer under the streetcar track, where the Town Creek flowed through Jackson and on into the Pearl River. Eudora, more determined than frightened, always

World War I: Curiosity

took their dare. Without fear, she would disappear into the small tunnel and follow the light at the end that led toward home.

Today, she headed home in the direction she came, with the cemetery in sight. Shadows were everywhere. Headstones in late afternoon cast elongated shadows that look like long fingers. Like the brick walk the chinaberry thrust upward, headstones of various sizes rose from the emerald ground. Carved deep into the stone were the names of those beneath the ground.

Eudora had found the white box in her mother's bureau completely by accident. As always, she removed the box with the long switch of russet hair stored in the bureau. She hung the tresses from a doorknob to brush and braid. One of her favorite stories was Rapunzel. She imagined this hair as her own. That day, Eudora noticed another box, a white cardboard box like the ones holding Chessie's engraved calling cards. Eudora forgot the stitch of hair. She forgot the brush. She took the box from the bureau.

Did she glance around to see if anyone was looking? Did she consider returning it to its place? How long did she hold the tightly closed box before daring to open it without permission? Curiosity was not something Eudora restrained.

The box held two buffalo head nickels. They lay side by side on a piece of white cotton. Excited about her newfound treasure, Eudora dashed to find her mother, open box in her hand. There was still time left in the day to run to the store. She found Chessie in another room. Eudora held the box up and asked if she could spend the nickels.

Chessie probably froze in that moment, confused, wondering, remembering the box. The memory of her oldest child surfaced. She snatched the box away from Eudora and snapped, "No!"

Eudora begged and cried to spend the nickels. "Why?" she asked. It was only two nickels.

Chessie gently pulled Eudora to her. She told Eudora about her older brother, Christian, who had died before Eudora was born. They buried him in the cemetery down the street. These two nickels were placed on his eyelids after he died. They were the only memory left of him.

Eudora's discovery in her mother's bureau uncovered stories. Within those stories were other stories. Floating between the lines were loss, guilt, regret and untold truths that felt much like lies. Eudora remembered her father's silver pocketknife scoring the bottom of her shoes. She remembered Chessie smothering the blazing Roman candle that flew up Eudora's sleeve. She remembered her mother blaming herself for the candle accident. Mostly, she remembered her parents' silence and their overprotection of Eudora, Edward and Walter. In between these lines was yet another story: the fear of losing another child.

Did Eudora view those coveted nickels, or any nickel, in the same light now? Each time Eudora headed toward the cemetery, would she search for her brother's headstone? When the cemetery was behind her, did she leave him behind, too? Or would his faceless ghost stir her fast-beating heart, even as she followed her shadow on the sidewalk back home?

Chapter 5
Segregation
Discovery

All over the nation, women and minorities made news. Margaret Sanger boldly breached obscenity laws by mailing out the *Woman Rebel*, her feminist newspaper informing women of social and economic news. In March 1916, she opened America's first birth control clinic. Carrie Belle Kearney, from Jackson's neighboring Madison County, fought fervently for women's suffrage. She spoke out for women's rights all over the nation. Her father had been a slaveholder when slavery was still legal. When speaking in the South, her argument for women's rights was to maintain white political supremacy and exclude from African Americans those same rights.[61] The year of Eudora's birth, W.E.B. Du Bois founded the National Association for the Advancement of Colored People (NAACP). He became the director of publicity and research, a member of the board of directors and editor of the *Crisis*, the NAACP monthly magazine.

A child in the segregated South couldn't help but notice things rarely talked about, signs that read, "Colored Waiting Room," "Colored seated in the rear," "Public Swimming Pool. Whites Only," "Colored Entrance" and "We Serve Colored, Carry Out Only." Since the freeing of slaves after the Civil War, there was a code in the South among white and black people:

The Inspiring Life of Eudora Welty

> *In Mississippi, any person...who shall be guilty of printing, publishing or circulating printed, typewritten or written matter urging or presenting for public acceptance or general information, arguments or suggestions in favor of social equality or of intermarriage between whites and negroes, shall be guilty of a misdemeanor and subject to fine not exceeding five hundred (500.00) dollars or imprisonment not exceeding six (6) months or both.*[62]

Because Eudora was never really around black people except those who were servants in a white household, including hers, she never really heard their conversations. That didn't mean she didn't watch and listen. No doubt, Eudora noticed the signs of compulsory separation and saw the contrast between white and black neighborhoods, between the white and black sides of town. She felt the pressure of invisible boundaries pushing like mighty gales before a storm.

Segregation: Discovery

Chessie had already cut out Eudora's dress, as well as Walter's and Edward's romper patterns, when their black seamstress, Fannie, arrived. As Fannie pinned the pattern onto Eudora, her fingers moved with ease and swiftness. Her stories about other Jackson families she sewed for erupted through the many pins protruding from her mouth, like pop fiercely shaken before opening. On her knees, she clumped around Eudora, telling her stories. She stuck a pin here and a pin there into the dress material. Eudora clutched at every word of Fannie's half-told stories, which Chessie interrupted.

"Fannie," Chessie said, "I'd rather Eudora didn't hear that."[63]

Fannie stopped that story but started another. Chessie chimed in again: "I think that will do, Fannie."

Gossip, as Chessie labeled these stories, was gossip, whether coming from Fannie or Chessie's lady friends. Chessie tolerated small talk but did not contribute. To Eudora, they were wonderful tales, like those in books. Scenes developed as with a turning page. The voice spoke first as a stranger but, by story's end, became that of an old friend. Eudora stored every word, as if one day she might use them herself.

Sundays were reserved for afternoon rides in the Welty vehicle. One of Chessie's friends usually rode along. Into the backseat Chessie, her friend and Eudora piled. Eudora hopped in the middle, where the conversation was always in her direction. Wind whooshed across the backseat. Eudora listened to one-sided conversations because Chessie rarely added to them. Every "he said" and "she said" became dialogue in the story. Declarations like "The crisis had come!" built the story to its climax.[64]

Out from under Chessie's watchful eyes and ears, Eudora craved more stories. To listeners, stories are everywhere. In Eudora's neighborhood, she sat at the feet of grand talkers while they shared old family stories. When visiting Clay County, West Virginia, she listened to the stories of her five uncles in the Andrews clan. The mountain songs they played on various instruments told stories. It was impossible to get Eudora to bed when her Uncles John, Moses, Carol, Edward and William plucked their banjos and sang songs like "Frog Went A-Courting and He Did Rise" or Chessie's favorite, "The West Virginia Hills." As Chessie tried fruitlessly, one brother would say, "Aw, Sister, let Girlie have her one more song."[65]

As a youngster, Eudora cherished her own tiny banjo, like her uncle's banjo. Chessie wanted Eudora to play a musical instrument, too. Sitting on a stool in the cowshed behind their North Congress home, Chessie milked their Jersey cow, thinking about that. While she funneled milk into quart bottles to be sold to her neighbors, the banjo wasn't the instrument she had in mind. She wanted Eudora to play piano.

Segregation: Discovery

Eudora was nine when Chessie bought her the Steinway upright piano. Every day, Eudora practiced her scales. She envisioned her mother perched on her own stool beside that old Jersey cow, milking away, listening for the voice of her mountain home and the flow of the river running through it.[66]

Visits to Chris's Ohio family home were so different from their visits to West Virginia. Here, there were no stories and very little conversation. At the end of the day, the only music came from a music box. They listened but didn't sing or dance. Strangely, in the parlor—where the shades were always drawn—was a pump organ no one ever played. This, of course, only made Eudora yearn for its voice. When alone, she opened the top and placed the tip of her finger against a key. It resisted her touch and remained silent. Of course, a pump organ must be pumped to produce sound. Then again, in this house, silence felt as normal as a forsaken organ.

Outside, the Hocking County hills rose and fell like ocean waves. Sounds of the crow's caw in the distance or Grandpa Welty working in the barn drew Eudora's attention. Here, Eudora played in the enormous Welty barn. She climbed on the furniture, crates, barrels and bales of hay. Smells of seed corn joined animal dander. Hens roosted in the bold buggy stored in the shadows where dust gathered. In Ohio, she relied on her imagination for stories. She created them from scenes around her. The horse peaking over its stall door reminded her of the horse Falada in the German story "The Goose Girl."

Grandpa Welty rarely spoke, especially to women or children in the house. Every so often, he sat on his wooden platform swing, pipe in his mouth and farm kitten in his lap. Eudora would go to him. He lifted her into his lap and let her hold the kitten. On Sundays, they traveled to church in the fine fringed buggy. In church, Grandpa Welty shed his usual quietness to lead the choir. His sonorous voice was full of gusto when singing to the Lord.[67]

Night returned you to the silence of the house and the lonely sound of the music box and the organ that never played. The organ belonged to Chris's real mother, who died when he was only a boy. Chris never talked about it. He wanted to forget the past, of which he never spoke. Like his timepieces, he wanted to move forward.

Eudora longed for unknown bits of the past. This silence ended up feeling to her also like a lie.[68]

A few years back, Chessie and Chris had taken Eudora out of school due to a fast-beating heart. From her parents' upstairs bedroom window, she watched her classmates at Davis School playing under Miss Duling's watchful eyes. At home, Chessie worked with Eudora on her spelling and arithmetic. It wasn't the same. Other kids at Davis may have been the majority, but they were leading normal, everyday routines. She lay confined to her bed, clinging to the sound of their laughter and even Miss Duling's bell.

At night, the house was still and sleepy. Tucked in her parents' bed, Eudora watched Chessie drape newspaper over the shade to darken the area around Eudora. Chessie tilted the lampshade, and light gathered on the two rockers across the room where she and Chris sat at the end of the day. Eudora listened for the hushed voices of her parents. Bathed in soft light, they rocked and quietly chatted but revealed no secrets.[69]

Chapter 6

Roaring Twenties

Expression

World War I ended. Progress was news. New York City's Grand Central, the world's largest railroad terminal, and the Panama Canal were open and in business. However, along with peace, progress and prosperity came the sinking of the *Lusitania*. There were cries for equality and independence. Labor strikes in the North for fair wages and good work conditions caused lockouts, injuries and even death. Up to half of the employed population worked twelve hours a day, often seven days a week, in unsafe, unsanitary conditions. They made barely enough in wages to survive in factory town shanties and the urban slums in which they lived.

By 1922, Mississippi's population had decreased by 6,500 residents. Since 1910, African Americans had outnumbered whites by 100,000. This number was rapidly decreasing with the great migration north to escape the Jim Crow South.[70] Entering the Roaring Twenties, newly elected Mississippi governor Lee M. Russell called for the ratification of the Nineteenth Amendment to the United States Constitution for women's suffrage. The Mississippi legislature refused to approve it. In fact, Mississippi was the last state to ratify the Nineteenth Amendment (in 1984). The federal amendment became effective in August 1920. Women voted for the first time in Mississippi in the 1920 presidential election. Republican

The Inspiring Life of Eudora Welty

Warren Harding defeated Democrat James Cox. Though nationwide Harding won 84 percent of the votes, he received fewer than 12,000 of the 82,351 votes in Mississippi.

Governor Russell increased appropriations for public education and started programs for hard-surfacing highways and conserving natural resources. He favored renovating the Governor's Mansion, going against former governor Theodore Bilbo's recommendation to sell it. The proposal was rejected to relocate the University of Mississippi from Oxford to Jackson. The legislature voted to increase the appropriations for the women's college in Columbus. The name of the college changed from Industrial Institute and College to the Mississippi State College for Women.

Lamar Life elected a new president, H.S. Weston. The company continued to prosper, expanding into Louisiana, Arkansas and Texas. All the while, Chris Welty climbed its ladder of success, often traveling to Chicago and New York on business trips.

Eudora filled her schedule with daily treks to the Jackson Public Library, one of the libraries partially funded by Andrew Carnegie. Chessie made it clear to the librarian, Miss Annie Parker, that Eudora could check out any book she wanted, except Elsie Dinsmore. Eudora, too often, became the heroine of the books she read. She slipped into the character's skin, as she had done when her brother dared her to go home by way of the storm sewer. Pretending to be Persephone in her six-month sojourn underground, Eudora crawled through the tunnel, clutching her mother's store order. In Elsie Dinsmore, Elsie faints and falls off her piano stool because her father made her practice at the piano for too long. Knowing her daughter's dramatics too well, Chessie said, "You're too impressionable, dear. You'd read that and the first thing you'd do, you'd fall off the piano stool."

Miss Annie Parker also made some things clear to Chessie. No more than two books could be checked out in a day. The proper layer of petticoats must be worn beneath dresses in her library. As much as it pained Eudora on both accounts, the library was something she wouldn't give up.[71] Eudora took some trips to the library on her bike. Others she took on her skates through the capitol building. In summer, warm breezes dampened her skin. She

ROARING TWENTIES: EXPRESSION

soared down the long flights of steps and steep terraces, past the Indian mummy inside the glass case in the Hall of Fame. Inside the rotunda of the capitol, the clack of her skates echoed off the curved walls and marble floor. This shortcut she took without her parents' permission. Perhaps she thought it better to risk doing something than risk losing the chance of not trying it at all.

Since her kindergarten days, Eudora had enjoyed art lessons. She sat with the other students at a small table drawing three daffodils freshly picked from the yard.[72] On certain days of the week, visiting teachers of the arts came to Davis School. The art instructor, Miss Ascher, was not as free-spirited as the singing teacher from up North, Miss Johnson. During a rare snowfall in Mississippi, Miss Johnson flung open the classroom window. In the hood of her cape, she captured snowflakes to show her students before they melted. Miss Ascher allowed the freedom of imagination and color. Yet her approval or disapproval of artwork materialized only through the sounds of "Hmm." Another art instructor during Eudora's early years was Jackson artist Marie Hull. She taught Eudora through

private lessons. Maybe she encouraged Eudora to submit her art to publications like the children's magazine *St. Nicholas*.[73]

Eudora used pen and ink for her piece *Heading for August*, a beachside vision of the ocean. On the beach, one child stands, peering out at two sailboats in the still water. Another, perched on his knees, plays in the sand, a small bucket to his left. A large beach umbrella lay on its side. Underneath the umbrella are two people barely visible. In bold print beneath the drawing is the word "AUGUST."[74]

Roaring Twenties: Expression

How long did she contemplate this picture with a critical eye before slipping it into an envelope? She mailed her drawing off to enter in Competition No. 245. Like any artist who submits work, Eudora must have anxiously awaited the response from the editor. As her mother sorted the mail, Eudora possibly peered over her mother's shoulder. Was there a letter for her today? Finally seeing her name, "Eudora Alice Welty," on the envelope, Eudora no doubt became excited. Unable to contain her curiosity, perhaps she snatched the letter from Chessie's hand. She opened the envelope and read the results:

> *The winners of Competition No 245: Gold Badges: Ruth Alden (age 14) New York; John Hull Whitcomb (age 13), Wisconsin; Silver Badges: Eudora Alice Welty (age 10), Mississippi; Dorothy Stephenson (age 16), Indiana; Justine Whittemore Chase (age 13), Connecticut.*

This was the first, but certainly not the last, award Eudora Alice Welty received as a young girl.[75]

To her friends, Eudora brought laughter and amusement. As small children, they had shared pony cart rides in the neighborhood. They learned to swim at the whites-only Pythian Castle public swimming pool and attended summer camp there.[76] At her house, she and her girlfriends sacrificed entire days to their paper dolls, creating and directing their performances. Her quick sense of humor probably fooled those who didn't know her well. She was actually very shy.[77]

On clear days, Eudora and her friends walked to the downtown theaters. They cut through Smith Park over to and down Capitol Street. They passed Pythian Castle and Lamar Life and crossed Town Creek. At the Majestic, they paid the five- or ten-cent admission. Claiming their usual box seats up front, they sat where the air was hot and stale. The location was perfect. The other cinema, the Istrione, was in an old livery stable. Once when watching Alice Brady dressed in her leopard skin in *Drums of Jeopardy*, a rat skittered over Eudora's feet. To someone like Eudora, a rat was little to suffer while stories burst to life on the big screen. Imagine Charlie Chaplin, Bea Lillie, Ed Wynn, the Marx Brothers and Eudora's idol, Mary Pickford.

The Inspiring Life of Eudora Welty

In the German film *The Cabinet of Dr. Caligari,* suspected murderer Cesare, dressed in black tights, inches his way along the wall out into the shadowy night. Terrifying to Eudora and her friends, screams and laughter filled the Istrione. After the movie, they went for sodas at McIntyre's Drugstore.

The Century Theatre, the first cinema to open in Jackson in 1901, was on Capital Street next door to the Medical Building. On this stage, Blackstone the Magician performed. In all his mysterious black-cape glory, he called for an eager child from the audience to assist him on stage. A powerful longing tugged at Eudora to go forward, but she would not sacrifice the safety of her chair for the stage.[78] This cinema hosted the traveling entertainers en route to New Orleans. Greats like Amelia Galli-Curci, an American-born Italian operatic soprano, and Paderewski, a virtuoso pianist, performed there. On some nights, Eudora attended the cinema in her mother's stead. Chessie enjoyed providing Eudora with the things she had never encountered as a girl, especially time with her father. Eudora yearned to enjoy being in a first-row balcony seat long after her bedtime. Thinking about her mother sitting alone in the corner of her room stirred Eudora with guilt. She imagined the lamp light casting shadows on her mother's creamy complexion while she slowly rocked, reading her Bible. What if her mother needed to refer to her concordance bound in worn leather? Usually someone fetched it for her when she called out, "Run, get me my concordance!"

Eudora learned that this was how Chessie wanted it. Tonight, her sons softly snored in their beds. Her daughter sat in her seat at the Century Theatre. To Chessie, the world was a dangerous place. Through the best intentions, Chessie protected her children. She would make sure her children saw the world as it was.[79]

Also given to Eudora were trips by train to New York and Chicago with her father. On her first trip to New York, Chris took Eudora to the Palace Theatre. This was the "palace among palaces," the deified vaudeville theater. Even Mary Pickford was discovered on the theater stage. Eudora so wanted to be like her favorite actress that she twisted wet sections of her hair into numerous rollers to later style into Mary Pickford curls.[80]

Roaring Twenties: Expression

As the train rolled, Eudora listened to the stories of strangers. She also watched them as her father's finger moved down the timetable and to the pocket watch he depended on. He pointed out to Eudora the mileposts placed along the tracks. They passed through a switch with the changing signal lights. He explained the semaphore, a system of visual signaling with two flags, one held in each hand, and the different positioning of the arms. The towns, people and landscapes created for Eudora canvases of scenes that stimulated her imagination. Even filling her father's collapsible drinking cup at the water cooler in the Pullman car touched her senses. The silver cup flavored the cool taste of water. She would always remember the smell and the taste. After supper in the dining car, Chris and Eudora trekked to the end of the train. They sat in folding chairs on the open-air observation platform and viewed the scenery. Sparks escaped from beneath the fast-moving train, lighting the darkness. The roar of the train drowns out the wildlife and insects hidden within the wood.[81] Eudora couldn't hear them, but she knew they were there. When she and her father tired, they entered their sleeper car. She pulled down the tightly tucked sheets of the bed. Snuggled between them, Eudora switched on the reading light to spotlight the book she read until her eyelids grew heavy. A small fan softly whirred and stirred the curtains.

Music, dance, art and writing play on the same field but in different positions. The rhythm of a story relies on sound, movement, vision and meaning. Eudora did them all. She danced. She played piano. She drew and painted. She wrote stories and poems. Like animals, children use their senses—seeing, hearing, speaking, smelling and touching—to explore their world.[82] Artists rediscover these senses. They re-create them for the world to embrace. Reading allowed Eudora to see the collaboration of words that develop character, plot and dialogue with intrigue and humor. Unlike music and art lessons, Eudora learned to write in the privacy of her room.

In 1921, Eudora read the newspaper advertisement in the *Memphis Commercial Appeal* inviting youth to enter a writing contest. The rules were to write a jingle in praise of Jackie Mackie Pine Oil, a household lubricant for sewing machines, squeaky hinges and other things.

The Inspiring Life of Eudora Welty

Advertising was the key to selling any product, even during the war. Billboards erected along roadsides drew attention from passersby. Later, they became debatable subjects for various women's groups. Jingles adorned the insides of streetcars, amusing their riders. In larger cities, jingles were displayed weekly in streetcars. Some actually told stories. The William Wrigley Company knew the importance of advertising and jingles. Its jingles were in newspapers, magazines and on the sides of downtown buildings. Famous artists like N.C. Wyeth and Norman Rockwell lent their artistic flair to advertising campaigns.[83]

Now, children Eudora's age were invited to create an advertising jingle of their own. Eudora had heard and possibly memorized many jingles of the era. As early as the age of nine, she understood how jingles sounded and worked. In Eudora's mind, a jingle, like a poem and a story, involved magic. For her jingle, Eudora turned Jackie Mackie into a magician who worked spells on all household tasks. This poem, too, she placed into an envelope, her mind surely thinking ahead to the contest's results. To any writer submitting her work, waiting and wondering is the hardest part. For Eudora, the wait would be well worth it.

Eudora's jingle won first prize, and she received a check for twenty-five dollars. Chessie exclaimed, "I'm not surprised." Her constant support built Eudora's confidence, but Eudora loved knowing that other people liked her writing, too. She felt her work had gone forth into the world, growing a life of its own. She explored artistic creation through the visual arts. Through practice and instruction, she improved her skills. She read and heard stories and then reenvisioned them. Eudora could not separate writing from reading. Both spring up, grow and come along together. Each story she read was her teacher.

Chapter 7
High School
Breaking Away

Eudora's seventh and last year at Duling School ended. The photographer snapped the graduating class—twenty-three boys, one who was barefoot, and fourteen girls. Eudora—her hair in braids around her head, adorned with ribbon—stood in the second row. The camera captured her smile and the brightness of her large, round eyes.[84]

Eudora thumbed through several magazines, probably the popular ones like *Life*, *Good Housekeeping*, *Vogue* and the *Ladies' Home Journal*. She needed the right words and photographs to create a book for Edward, who was sick in bed. She had decided on a tragedy about protagonist Fitzhugh Green and his wife, Lallie. They would take a journey on a nifty little bike. The antagonists were the delegation from the weather bureau and Delegate McGooflenish. To ensure rising conflict, Eudora added a few lions, tigers, insects, dogs, bears and a large bird named Carolyn among the cattails to draw Lallie's eye.

The book *The Glorious Apology*, by E. Welty, reveals Eudora's fascinating humor and imagination and her familiarity and ease with building a story. For instance, in the introduction of the book, she borrowed two excerpts from the magazines she searched and put them together to make "What Spell Does This Strange Book

The Inspiring Life of Eudora Welty

Cast Over Its Readers: A Flaming story of the men who tame rivers of steel—How one of them seared the craven fear from his soul." Additionally, she put her best foot forward in her first foray into "professional publishing." For any publisher, sales are the utmost goal. At a young age, Eudora was writer and "publisher" of this book. To accomplish this moneyed goal, Eudora cut out the phrase "Your Name in Gold" and pasted it above "—on this Wonderful Book" on the introduction page. She then wrote beneath the entries: "For every 10 purchases."[85]

During the '20s, advertising reached a new height. High-paid advertising agencies knew how to handle fierce competition among sellers of manufactured goods and retail merchandise. Advertising agencies created and placed ads. They also named, packaged, priced and promoted the products' distribution. Ads also reached another level. They used psychology to draw on the emotions of buyers, not statistics or data on how strongly a product was manufactured. Their strong characters lived out their fantasies through the product. Ads told stories of freedom and excitement. Prospective buyers, both male and female, contemplated how it felt to drive away into the sunset in the advertised car, the wind blowing, tousling their hair.

Ads even emotionalized bad breath. Some conjured scenes of women forced to live alone because of halitosis. They read something like:

> *Oh, memories that bless and burn…Sometimes, when lights are low, they come back to comfort and at the same time sadden—those memories of long ago, when she was a slip of a girl in love with a dark-eyed Nashville boy. They were the happiest moments of her life—those days of courtship…And then, like a stab, came their parting…the broken engagement… the sorrow and the shock of it. Are you sure about yourself? LISTERINE ends halitosis.*

Advertisements like these certainly drew Eudora's attention, and her chuckles, as she found words and phrases for *The Glorious Apology* to add to her own words. On one page, after the huge yellow bird named Carolyn snatches Lallie up in her long bill and swallows her,

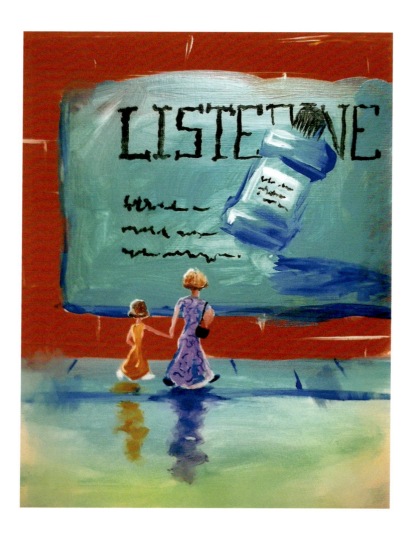

Eudora included the cutout phrase of a mouthwash ad that read, "Gargling alone is not enough!"

To begin chapter one, Eudora wrote: "'Alas,' murmured Fitzhugh Green to the admiring public. 'What else is there left in life?' There was no answer." In chapter three, she wrote, "'Darling,' breathed Lallie. 'What would I do without you?' (See illustration)." The illustration was a photo of a woman holding a handsome man. She gave Edward the book in 1921.

The Inspiring Life of Eudora Welty

This would not be the only booklet she created at home. Chessie kept these early stories, along with Eudora's artwork, safely stored away. From magazine to film, stories of every genre and category captivated Eudora. The more she read and saw, the more she craved, as receiver and creator.

The year of *The Glorious Apology*, Eudora entered eighth grade at Jackson Central High School, a brick building on Northwest Street near the new capitol. There, compositions concentrated on themed exercises. Teachers severely criticized writing for grammatical mistakes. Eudora was later thankful for strict instruction and expectations of excellence. Still, it was the simple narrative assignments like what she did on vacation that enthusiastically pulled her to pen and paper. She loved informal writings focusing on people and their lives. Unlike her friends, who dreaded the book report, Eudora thrilled in the task of retelling a story in her own words. She added her thoughts and opinions. She enjoyed it so much that she wrote book reports for those who didn't read the book.

One of Eudora's close friends wrote a report on a book that didn't exist. The English teacher had complained to Nash Burger about his habitual selection of Edgar Rice Burroughs and Zane Grey. Nash decided to write his book report on an author nobody knew, not even his teacher. They had been studying "L'Allegro" and "Il Penseroso" in class when Nash conjured up his fictitious author, Milton C. Milton, and the plot. Only his friends, including Eudora, were aware of the hoax. The teacher and class well received Nash's book report. After he delivered his report, Eudora raised her hand and asked if Nash could bring the book to school so she could read it. Nash agreed but, of course, forgot to bring the nonexistent book. Each time Nash forgot, Eudora publicly reminded him. The joke remained among Nash, Eudora and the other students who knew the book was a phony.[86]

Many of Eudora's neighborhood friends attended Jackson Central, too—Davis schoolmates like Jane Percy Slack, Willia Wright and Sonny Withers, whose horse cart Eudora often rode on the sidewalk. Her Davis School friends from different neighborhoods were Nash Burger and Ralph Hilton. New friends included John Robinson, from the Mississippi Delta, and Lehman Engel, a Jew

High School: Breaking Away

who felt somewhat lost in a predominantly southern Christian atmosphere. These classmates built lifelong friendships.

Having already won two prizes, one in art and one in writing, Eudora's work in both areas flourished during her high school years. Jackson Central's yearbook, *The Quadruplane*, welcomed and published her work. *Jackson Hi-Life*, the school newspaper did, too. In 1923, two of her pen-and-ink illustrations portrayed gnomes wearing pointed hats and romping around on large books. The titles she wrote neatly in Old English script. In the illustration entitled "Foreword," the gnomes appear to be workers opening the book for viewers. In the illustration entitled "Finis," the gnomes are closing the book, as if their work is done. She drew the gnomes in active positions, climbing and pointing, leaning and sitting, tugging and falling. The lifelike faces of the gnomes were striking. Maybe Eudora drew the realistic faces of the gnomes from people she knew. Her "Court Jester" illustration was also published that year. She drew a picture of a king with a protruding round belly perched on his throne. His court jester stands before him with a large feather, tickling the king's nose. Both wear wide grins. It took great skill to illustrate personalities through drawings.

Her sights for a publisher, even at this young age, progressed far beyond her school and hometown. She again contributed to *St. Nicholas* magazine, which published the works of Edna St. Vincent Millay, Ring Lardner and Rachel Larson. This time, she submitted a poem entitled "Once Upon a Time." The success of her Jackie Mackie entry and the judges' encouragement might have influenced Eudora's decision to submit writing this time in lieu of art. Her reference to "St. Nick" could have influenced the editors in selecting it. After all, the name of the magazine was *St. Nicholas*. The *Commercial Appeal Memphis* selected Eudora's pen-and-ink submissions for its children's page. Doubtless, she had studied illustrations, articles and stories in different publications. She noted comparisons and differences in the work of others. She made mental notes of what she liked and did not like. Her early publication accomplishments make it obvious that she was aware of submission guidelines. What may be difficult to comprehend is Eudora's passion as a young girl to express so vibrantly and frequently. Even her Jackson Central classmates and teachers listened in awe of her stories. They were smooth and painstakingly written. They veered without warning into quiet humor. She deftly described her characters and scenes in a way that made listeners step into the story with her.[87]

Eudora, like her mother, challenged tradition. Unlike many Jackson women in her social circle, Chessie had gone to work at an early age to help take care of her family. To her brothers, she had been a second mother. This upbringing instilled a distinct quality of ambition and drive in Chessie. She paid her way through college in the early 1900s, when most women did not go to college. She was outspoken and unafraid to speak her mind. She disagreed with mission work in foreign countries trying to change other cultures by telling them what to believe and how to believe it. She was dismayed with women's social groups designed only for dressing up to share pleasantries and refreshments. In spite of this, Chessie, no doubt, understood the need for women's clubs that cropped up after World War I. She supported groups that studied literature and culture to expand intellect and enhance self-improvement. Women desired more and more to get out of the house. They became socially and even politically involved. Clubs gave them the ability and platform to do so. Chessie joined the Research Club. In 1922, she helped found Jackson's Woman's Club. She involved herself mainly in the aspects of gardening and conservation.[88]

Similarly, Eudora was not interested in being a cheerleader. She did join the Yeller Club, which supported and cheered the teams at every game. Club members had to create an original yell for each game. This was no problem for Eudora. She, nonetheless, leaned toward literary and drama clubs. She was literary editor for the *Jackson Hi-Life* and served as secretary of the Dramatic Club. She performed many roles for school productions. Even with all her extracurricular activities, Eudora maintained honor roll status. She and her friends wrote plays and staged them in the garage with Walter and Edward. Their audience consisted of neighbors and family members.

In 1924, Jackson Central added a twelfth grade. To ensure a graduating class for that year, the school chose sixty students to take extra credit each year to graduate a year early in 1925. Eudora was one of them.[89]

Family time for the Weltys included early morning swims and lectures, concerts and plays in Smith Park brought by the Circuit Chautauqua. On summer nights, the Weltys gathered in the park with other neighborhood friends. Spreading quilts on the grass, they drank lemonade while being entertained. Named after the series of festivals held on Lake Chautauqua in western New York State, summer Chautauqua shows came to ten thousand towns in the United States. They played for a week. This "great forum of culture and inspiration," former president Theodore Roosevelt called the "most American thing in America." Over forty million people were entertained through the Chautauqua circuits. As Eudora and her brothers played on the grounds, Chris and Chessie listened to yodelers, Hawaiian crooners and brass band concerts performing selections from William Tell and other orchestras. The children stopped their play to watch a magician perform magic tricks. Afterward, as the inspirational lecturer stepped up to the podium to speak on personal success, they returned to play.

THE INSPIRING LIFE OF EUDORA WELTY

The clay banks of Terry Road in South Jackson had deep indentions carved into them like caves. The children climbed and explored these banks while parents visited with one another. When visiting the Civil War military park in Vicksburg, the Weltys often included their friends to picnic on the grounds. Eudora, Edward and Walter mounted the cannons, pausing long enough to allow Chris to snap a photo. In summer, Chessie also took Eudora and her brothers to Hubbard Wells, a small resort. There, healthful waters flowed, and paper lanterns hung from the trees. In the evening, a local pianist played music. After a long workweek, Chris joined them on the weekend.

Activities and the scenery fed Eudora's imagination. She recorded her experiences in her memory. One such memory would surface years later: "the farm lying quite visible, like a white stone in water, among the stretches of deep woods in their colorless dead leaf."[90] The memory had lain in waiting for her.

As a young girl, Chessie made Eudora take piano lessons. Though Chessie found the lessons important, Eudora loved listening to music more than playing it. Nevertheless, Chessie wanted her daughter to play and to play well. After all, she had grown up with her brothers' variety of instruments and songs. On the afternoon of one piano recital, Eudora's parents and family sat in the audience. However, something else weighed heavily on Chessie's and Chris's minds and hearts. They did not want to worry their children. That afternoon, they had something else planned. Under a shield of secrecy, Chris and Chessie headed to the hospital after the recital. They thought it best not to worry the children. Chessie underwent surgery for breast cancer. Eudora did not learn of her mother's cancer and surgery until she was grown.[91]

In the early 1920s, residences in and around Eudora's downtown neighborhood had declined. Many became multi-family rental homes. In 1923, the Weltys bought a lot on the Pinehurst gravel road. Across the street was the large wooden building known as Belhaven College, built in 1883. About 1910, man and oxen cleared the Pinehurst suburb. The city extended the trolley line running north of Jackson. This made the area easily accessible and attractive to prospective buyers and builders. Chessie missed the mountains

HIGH SCHOOL: BREAKING AWAY

of her West Virginia home so much that Chris chose a lot that rose slightly. He tried to convince Chessie that their new home would sit on a hill. Chris's idea of a hill and Chessie's were completely different. While the lot was being prepared for construction, the Weltys moved into a rental house in the area. In the nearby lake, Edward and Walter often skinny-dipped.[92]

Chris, now general manager and vice-president of Lamar Life, oversaw the construction of Lamar Life's new office building. This would be Jackson's first skyscraper, a Gothic building of white marble. Thirteen stories high, gargoyles would guard its clock tower and stone alligators its front entrance.[93]

For Chris, each day must have presented new opportunities. People say that an optimist looks forward to what can be. A pessimist looks at what could have been. Chris and Chessie kiddingly accepted their roles of optimist and pessimist, respectively. On one summer trip to West Virginia and Ohio, the family was taking the ferry across the river. Eudora, saw the frayed rope used to pull the ferry. She asked if it was going to break before they made it to the other side. To relieve Eudora's fear, Chris asked the ferryman, "It's never broken before, has it?"

To which the ferryman replied, "No, sirree."

Chris turned to Eudora and said, "You see? If it never broke before, it's not going to break this time."

Chris believed that whatever happened, good or bad, worked out in the end. Chessie, however, disagreed.

"You're such an optimist, dear," she said.

"You're a good deal of a pessimist, sweetheart."

"I certainly am," replied Chessie.[94]

The new Welty home outside the bustling city would offer fresh air and open spaces, giving Chessie the outdoor space she needed for her gardens. They selected plans for a two-story, Tudor Revival house of stucco and brick with steep roofs and plenty of tall, narrow windows. Chris managed the plans of both the house and the new Lamar office building with architect Wyatt C. Hedrick of Fort Worth, Texas. Chessie concentrated on her garden spaces that she would plant around their new home. One time, the house plan interfered with Chessie's garden plan. Chris wanted the driveway to enter the property from a side street rather than from the front. This meant the driveway would split the backyard, interrupting Chessie's garden scheme. Chris changed the plans so that the driveway entered from Pinehurst Street in front.[95]

Many new houses cropping up in the suburbs had flower gardens. Chessie spent much time learning about plants, their origins and how they developed.[96] Avid gardeners like Chessie believed that exposure to outdoor scenery improved physical health and lifted spirits. They also believed gardens counteracted harmful consequences of fast-paced living and frenzied nerves. Though a pessimist, Chessie was optimistic for the gardens around their new home. Life does move forward. With the progression of time comes the chance to start over.

Moreover, the Weltys were expecting another child.

Chapter 8
Flappers and Jazz
Transformation

Eudora entered her teens during the First Youth Rebellion in the United States. Young people began to question authority and seek independence after the long, grueling war. Hobble skirts and long hair were out. Shorter skirts worn with silk stockings were in. Fake jewelry and cloche hats were hot items in women's fashion. Modern young women were called "flappers." Jazz seized the music industry and developed its own language, terms like:

- baloney or banana oil: both mean nonsense
- bee's knees, berries or cat's meow: all mean something superb or wonderful
- cake-eater: ladies' man
- cheaters: eyeglasses
- ritzy: elegant (from the "Ritz," the Paris hotel)
- the real McCoy: genuine article
- heebie-jeebies: the jitters
- speakeasy: a saloon or bar selling bootleg whiskey

Many more terms accompanied the age. Modern dances were the shimmy, the Charleston and the black bottom. All were said to cheapen womanhood. The *Southern Baptist* publication stated that change among the youth "causes grave concern on the part of all who have the ideals at heart of purity and home life and the stability

of our American civilization." However, girls craved liberation from corsets and layers of slips. Mothers forced their daughters to wear girdles, especially to parties. When the daughters arrived at the parties, they rushed into restrooms and "parked their girdles."[97]

With the close of the holiday season, Christmas decorations were neatly stored away for the next year. Concentration returned to the new Pinehurst house, laying out the garden spaces and preparing for the new baby. Chris returned to overseeing the construction of the Lamar Life building. Often, the whole family crowded into the car, and Chris drove them downtown to the see the progress of the building. They all climbed the fire escape to the top of the building to gaze out over Jackson. Fall brought cooler winds; winter brought cold gales that stung your eyes. The city was constantly changing, with new buildings and the paving of roads. The old and familiar, like the Old Capitol, Governor's Mansion and city hall, remained tributes to a past of perseverance and determination. The change that Jackson saw was good.

However, you cannot always neatly plan and arrange change. Nor is some change welcomed. Of this, Chris and Chessie were well aware. In the end, some changes you cannot control.

On the night of January 26, 1924, Chris and Chessie rushed to the hospital, where their premature daughter was stillborn. The next day, they buried Eudora's baby sister. Sorrow once again seized Chris and Chessie.

Even in Mississippi, the coldness of January seeps beneath the cracks of doors and through windowpanes. Nothing grows in winter. Branches are bare, and flower bulbs rest below the ground, waiting for spring. Being caught between residences must have been difficult for them during this grieving season. The home at 741 North Congress had sheltered the Welty family for many years. Though one child had died there, three were born there, bringing squeals of laughter, constant chatter and quick footfalls slapping against the wooden floors. For Eudora's family, there had been unspeakable memories. There were also good memories, many good memories. These surely helped Chris focus as he proceeded into the future. Chessie still grieved. She seemed to latch on to the past, wondering why some babies had to die.

Spring did come, leaving winter in its wake. Everything grew green again. Chris had planned a special West Coast trip for his top insurance agents and their wives. He had always been the traveler in the family. He made sure business trips were never mere business trips but also opportunities to explore new places and new sights. Eudora occasionally tagged along. However, this time Chessie was joining Chris and the others on the train trip across America. She had enlisted a family friend to care for Eudora, Edward and Walter during their absence. A trip of this magnitude required extensive

planning. Chris chartered two special Pullmans for the group of forty-five scheduled to go by train. They would travel to New Orleans to board the westbound train to Los Angeles, the location of the annual convention of national life underwriters. Chessie had bought her wardrobe for the trip. As the trip grew nearer, lively conversations about the upcoming adventure perhaps went around the dinner table. However, the day before the trip, Chessie backed out. Eudora would go instead.

The summer of 1924, Eudora boarded the train with her father. Destination: California. Because they had not planned on Eudora going on the trip, in New Orleans Chris took Eudora shopping, buying her everything she needed. Afterward, they departed on the train heading west.[98]

This trip went beyond her father's usual business trips, with a night at the theater or a day at the museum in Chicago or New York. This trip included Juarez, Mexico, and the Grand Canyon. Eudora had only heard about these places. Chugging across America, outside the window the scene changed drastically. Lush green woodlands and gentle rolling fields of the eastern states changed into the West's miniature junipers, pinyon and ponderosa pines, aspens and sagebrush. Brilliantly red canyons dropped violently. Rock hills climbed steeply and resembled windowless, uninhabitable buildings in the middle of nowhere. At first sight, western landforms appear stark and lonely. Then they become brilliant and colorful. In the distance, rugged cowboys herd their steer across the plains.

Once Chris and Eudora arrived at the hotel in Los Angeles, Eudora freshened up by washing her hair. At an open window, she brushed her hair while the wind blew it dry. Breathing in the Pacific air from her room high above, she viewed the sights. Home was far away and the pleasures of travel before her. As the Pacific air caressed her skin, Eudora pondered the purchase of this trip through her mother's sacrifice—again.[99]

The Lamar Life group ventured to Venice Beach. They toured the sights of Los Angeles. After the convention, the group returned home by way of San Francisco, Reno, Salt Lake City, Colorado Springs and Pike's Peak. At his Lamar Life office, Chris assembled and published a booklet entitled *To the Golden Gate and Back Again*. In it, he featured six of Eudora's illustrations. Chris included details of the trip. The section "As Told by Others" consisted of letters from the other trip participants. Eudora most likely wrote the one from "Punk Clabberneck of Podunk, Mississippi."[100]

Chessie threw herself into planning the Pinehurst landscape. She made lists of plants and shrubs for the yard. To get the best effects, you should have a complete picture in your mind at least, but it's even better on paper—before the house is even built. Thus, the house, garden and landscape blend as one.[101] Chris returned to overseeing the construction of their new home and the Lamar Life building. For Eudora, it must have seemed as though something new was replacing everything old in her life. Even Jackson Central was adding the new junior and senior high school building. Eudora worked in her classrooms to the sound of hammers and saws. To Eudora, the buildings, both new and old, represented youth and age, and as she pondered this, she wrote.

Her piece for *The Quadruplane*, "Youth and Age," created dialogue between the young and old buildings. The new building, filled with hope and ambition, dominates the world the two buildings share. The old building still stands but fades away into the shadow of the new, into memories.

As Eudora's work matured, it grew seasoned with the flavors of satire and irony. She wrote a parody, "The Conference Condemns Caroline." The student Caroline is too exhausted from extracurricular activities to concentrate on schoolwork. A committee of Latin civics and physics, geometry and literature figures confront her. They warn her that procrastination of lessons becomes more difficult as subjects get harder. The character Caroline clearly represents Eudora in the story.

Like Miss Duling at Davis School, Jackson Central High principal John Luther Roberts expected order and decorum in the halls and classrooms. Coach and principal Roberts had been an athlete at Mississippi College. He ran every morning through his neighborhood. At his school, the Boys Hi-Y and Girls Hi-Y met weekly to read the Bible and say prayers. At Hi-Y assemblies, many clergymen spoke on morality and purity. They hoped to steer the youth onto the right path leading to their futures.[102]

Something about the Hi-Y Club bothered Eudora, but after much hesitation, she joined. The club awarded points for doing "good." It held candlelight ceremonies to honor a member's progress through various achievements, like the Golden Circle, the first achievement. Here, a wire ring representing purity was presented to the member. In turn, the member vowed to wear the ring through youth, marriage and old age, even unto death. In Eudora's mind, the Jackson Central teacher in charge of the club was trying to brainwash girls into believing a kiss was a sinful act. The teacher told how one young girl who surrendered a kiss was forever cursed. Wherever her lips touched, a black mark rose on her skin. Eudora was not one easily led astray. She had never been kissed, but she undeniably knew girls who had. Their skin was as white and pure as hers was.

Eudora was captivated—obsessed, really—with Latin. She started a club devoted to it: the Girgil Club. She lived by its motto:

Listen, cram and be careful,
for eighth period you may read.

Eudora's choices for the Girgil Club's colors (black and blue) and the club book (*The Aeneid*) reveal her inclination toward satire. She found humor in most everything. Members of the Girgil Club consisted of senior girls who ate lunch during sixth period. They read their Virgil lesson at the very last minute, which was no problem for Eudora. Top students, like Nash Burger, whose mother enlisted college graduate Annie Virden to tutor him on Cicero, depended on Eudora's assistance in translating Latin. In fact, Latin came so easy to Eudora that she often read something else during class.[103]

Enamored with Latin, Greek and the mythology she had read as a child, Eudora wrote the piece "The Origin of Shorthand." In this story, the Greek Cubedites, *Parthenon Press*'s star reporter, wears the disguise of a Roman toga and attends a Roman forum where Cicero is speaking. Cubedites invents the first shorthand so he will not be caught writing in the Greek language.

Her senior year, Eudora ventured into creating crossword puzzles that were quickly becoming the rage. Her puzzles, too, had Greek themes. The answers were filled in around the big, bold, black letters: JHS. One of her clues was "The Greek who was always ready for Saturday night." ANSWER: Archimedes. Richard L. Simon and M. Lincoln Schuster (later known as Simon & Schuster) first published crossword books. Baltimore and Ohio Railroads provided dictionaries on their trains for the passengers' convenience in working crossword puzzles. Various types of competitions were growing across the country as well, like dance marathons, cross-country races and rocking chair derbies.

In January 1925, Eudora submitted her poem "In the Twilight," a tribute to the moon ("The Queen of the Night shyly peeping o'er the hill"), to *St. Nicholas* magazine. This piece won a Silver Badge. Several of her art pieces served as dividers in *The Quadruplane*. "Olympic Games" divided the sports section; "First Estate" was the divider page for the freshman class; "Second Estate," the divider for the sophomore class; "Third Estate," the divider for the junior class; and "Fourth Estate," the divider for the senior class. She drew the illustration for Nash Burger's fictitious club the "Junior Jupiter Juvenile Detective Agency." Nash also worked on the school paper, along with Eudora and their friend William Calvin Wells Jr. While Nash wrote serious pieces on loyalty and duty, he was also named the "Joke Editor." For *The Quadruplane*, he created "Dead-Eye Dick," a comic tale of western derring-do.[104]

Eudora also illustrated her Girgil Club page, including its officers (president, Ruth Gainey; vice-president Beth Heidelberg; secretary, Dorothy Simmons; treasurer, Willie Sullivan) and members (Beth Enochs, Mary Flowers Jackson, Annie McNair, Virginia Vance and Eudora Welty). She illustrated the music, "Early Explorers," "The Oracle Speaks" and history sections as well.

At her senior Hi-Y Banquet, Eudora rebelled in her own way against the club and her teacher's obvious propaganda. She performed in the light burlesque *Wild Nell, the Pet of the Plains* and entered the gum-chewing contest afterward. That spring, she played Peggy Woofers in *Three Live Ghosts*. Her energy never seemed to wane. No one ever grew tired of her or her work. In fact, in Eudora's senior year, her classmates liked her so much that they voted her "Demeter," which means Most Dependable, and "Irene," meaning she was "Best All 'Round." The April 30, 1925 *Jackson Hi Life* article, "What They Intend to Do," had "author" typed beneath Eudora's name.[105]

Eudora, like her father, set her sights ahead and outside Jackson, Mississippi. Travels with her father had given her a taste of what was out there. She had an intense need to be independent. However, Eudora had graduated a year early. Chris and Chessie were not ready for her to be on her own. They preferred that she attend Millsaps College, near their Pinehurst home. Eudora, on the other hand, was determined to leave Jackson. They compromised on the Mississippi State College for Women in Columbus, Mississippi.[106]

FLAPPERS AND JAZZ: TRANSFORMATION

The Pinehurst house was not finished, but Chessie was thrilled with her garden. She set up Eudora's "al fresco" graduation party on the lawn on a Wednesday afternoon at five thirty. She invited the 1925 graduating class of Central High School. Jane Percy Slack tended the huge punch bowl set atop a bed of flowers. For her party, Eudora divided the lawn into two areas: Babyland, where they played kid games, and Land of the Grown Ups, where anyone found acting dignified or grownup had to go. To return to Babyland, they had to perform a stunt to get out of Land of the Grown Ups.[107]

On July 19, the Weltys took a long trip to Trout Lake, Wisconsin, before heading to Chicago to meet Grandpa Welty. They purchased Eudora's clothes for college. After driving Grandpa Welty back home, they headed for West Virginia to spend time with the Andrews clan.

Eudora enjoyed very little time in her new home on Pinehurst Road before moving to Columbus, two hundred miles north. Mississippi State College for Women (MSCW), known as "the W," was the first state college in the country for women. Maud Butler, William Faulkner's mother, had attended the college when it was the Industrial Institute and College. The mother of soon-to-be-acclaimed playwright and Mississippian Tennessee Williams, who was attending high school in St. Louis, walked to the W campus to take voice lessons.[108]

Eudora Welty, now a sixteen-year-old girl, stepped onto the campus. Her sights directly on her literary future, she immediately set out to find the college newspaper.[109]

Chapter 9
College Years
The Journey

As planned and promised, Eudora attended the W for two years; along with her were 1,200 other girls from all over Mississippi. Under the college's strict rules, watchful eyes kept up with every student's comings and goings. There were six registers: one to sign before leaving campus, one before leaving Columbus, one before going on dates, one before spending the night out and one before going to the college hospital. The last register was for guests to sign in and out. Although a state college, students were required to attend chapel twice a week. In the overcrowded space of the chapel, sometimes a student fainted during the fifteen-minute "Alma Mater." Girls were required to wear conservative navy blue uniforms to town and to campus functions. The spring uniform was a one-piece silk dress or a woolen skirt with a crepe-de-chine blouse. In winter, they wore a one-piece woolen dress and a long separate coat or a conservative plain coat suit. The W banned all "flapper" attire. In fact, hems could be no shorter than ten inches from the floor. Sleeves were to be no shorter than nine inches from the armhole. Students should always wear hats off campus. Shoes with low heels were preferred and French heels discouraged.

As a freshman, Eudora roomed in Old Main, a pre–Civil War building constructed in 1860. The building's fire escape was an iron standpipe with a tin chute. It had corkscrew turns and openings at each floor. The chute was a quick way to class or an escape into night before the whistle blew and the gates were locked. Often, Eudora slipped down and out of the tunnel. She longed to be transported to somewhere distant, far from the small town of Columbus. The words from William Alexander Percy's poem "Home" bounced about in her mind: "I have a need of silence and of stars/Too much is said too loudly. I am dazed."[110]

She found comfort, as always, in the words of other authors while using her own to write editorials as the only freshman reporter with the college paper, the *Spectator*. The *Spectator* evidently needed Eudora. Only two months after her arrival, the November 14, 1925 edition read:

> *I defy anyone,* Ladies Home Journal, *Billy and William included, to be more alive or more in evidence on this particular stamping ground of the flowers of Mississippi than Eudora Welty. I stand back in amazement at the things that woman does. Anybody want posters drawn? Page Eudora—she'll dash you off an exceedingly effective one in no time at all. Somebody to collect annual money? Eudora will do it. Something clever and funny for the* Spec? *That's the best thing she does. Someone for the Dramatic Club Play? Why, faith and 'begorra, here's Eudora again—absolutely perfect as wheezing, sneezing, pleasing Miss Trimble in* The Rector…[111]

The *Spectator* published Eudora's pieces "Burlesque Ballad," "The Great Pinnington Solves the Mystery," "Autumn's Here," "The Gnat," "'I' for Iris—Irma, Imogene," "The Fairy Crepe," "Desire," "I Could Show You the Colors," "Incident" and "Prophecy," as well as her illustrations. She served on the annual staff of *Meh Lady*, where she also worked as photographer. She founded the comic magazine *Oh, Lady*, in which she also included her illustrations. She was cast in a play put on by the Dramatic Club.

Her longing for independence, nevertheless, grew stronger. Unlike the constraints at her Hi-Y Club, which she silently resisted, the constraints at the W she tested and broke. Once in December,

College Years: The Journey

Eudora and her friends Anna Lou White, May Risher, Katie Davidson, Frances Davis, Dana Davis, Earline Robinson and Lois Prophet walked fifteen miles to the abandoned antebellum mansion called Waverly. They carried food, a coffeepot and packs of cigarettes stashed away in their sweater pockets. This was not the first time they made this trek. It would not be the last.

They ferried across the Tombigbee River that flowed south through Aberdeen and Columbus Lake reservoirs, past Columbus. At the railroad trestle, all the girls, except Eudora, hesitated in fear of crossing. Eudora boldly crossed the narrow iron pathway, leading her friends like children to the other side.

The Waverly mansion rose like the hundred-year-old boxwood bushes lining the way to the entrance. An icehouse still stood on the property. The cemetery held the ghosts of Waverly, along with overgrown grass and weeds. Inside, though empty of people, there were dusty items. Fishing poles hung in the entryway, waiting for a steady, patient hand to take them down to the river. Mother-of-pearl keys on the piano placed against the wall invited beckoning young fingers to try a song. Two circular stairways led to the upstairs locked bedrooms. Downstairs was much more inviting. The bedrooms, one on each side of the entry hall, were open for view. Clothes still lay on the canopy beds, ready for someone to slip into them. A set of Sir Walter Scott's Waverly books resided on the library shelves along with the other books.

Eudora also discovered other ways to leave campus without being chaperoned—sometimes to places the W had deemed off limits, like the Gilmer Hotel dining room. Eudora won a Charleston contest at the Princess Theatre. For a girl overprotected all her life, Eudora turned out some daring feats. She wrote to the Hershey Company explaining how she and the girls at MSCW were starving in Mississippi. Could the Hershey Company please send some chocolates? The company mailed Eudora a case of chocolate.[112]

Although Eudora longed to leave the W, she discovered people from different cultures and backgrounds. They possessed different opinions and beliefs. They were from diverse social and economic statuses. She noted that even though they were all Mississippians, their accents and customs varied according to their home regions in the state. This expanded her world beyond Jackson. Still, she wanted more. What she wanted was outside Mississippi.

After Eudora completed her two years at the W, Chris and Chessie felt more ready to let Eudora go. Plus, she was eighteen now. Two colleges accepted her application: Randolph-Macon Woman's College in Virginia and the University of Wisconsin. Some of her MSCW credits would not transfer to Randolph-Macon, the college she preferred. She decided on the University of Wisconsin.

Wisconsin exposed Eudora to things she had never experienced at the W. In the art class, she sat at her easel. A young female model, situated a little above them, stood and dropped her robe. She posed nude for the class. Eudora had never painted a human body in this way. Her teacher suggested she go to the library and practice drawing the statues.[113] English professor Ricardo Quintana thought Eudora brilliant in the literary sense. He introduced her to the work of John Donne and Jonathan Swift. However, Quintana's belief in her did little to spur her writing efforts in Wisconsin.[114]

Eudora roomed in a tall, narrow, three-story building at 625 North Frances, only two houses away from Lake Mendota. The house held to the rules of the campus dormitories. Weekday curfews were 10:00 p.m. Weekend curfews were 12:30 a.m. Eudora's room was on the third floor, at the end of the hall. Her single room held her bed, a filled bookcase and the red Royal portable typewriter her father had given her.[115] Each floor had one bathroom and a telephone that everyone on the floor shared. Often, she helped the other girls get ready for their dates and a night on the town. To some of the girls, Eudora was reserved and shy. To others, she was brilliant, charming and quiet.[116] Her naïvety kept her from fully participating in this era of freedom women were discovering. She did manage to break a few rules by drinking a little "bathtub gin" and "needle beer" during this Prohibition era.

Her first roommate from the W, Dana Davis, also attended Wisconsin. She left after one semester. Eudora made other friends. For Christmas 1928, she traveled to Montana with a friend to work for her father's newspaper. Her experience there spurred her later short story "A Piece of News."[117] To Eudora, Wisconsin girls seemed like "sticks of flint living in an icy world."[118] This, added to feeling misplaced and alone, possibly crushed her normally lighthearted, comic spirit around other people. It also squashed her enthusiasm to write. At Jackson Central and the W, Eudora had been absorbed in literary and art activities. At the University of Wisconsin, Eudora isolated herself from drama and literary organizations. Her poem "Shadows" was the only piece published in the *Wisconsin Literary Magazine*.

Nash Burger, who had always thought Eudora an incredible writer, told her, "You will be famous with your novel one day." He asked her to submit a story to the college magazine *Hoi-Polloi*, on which he and George Stephenson, who was also from Jackson, worked. She submitted an illustration rather than a poem or story. He sometimes sent Eudora his stories for comment. One was about a black firefighter. His stoking of the fire in a steamboat boiler had flames leaping in "plutonic glee." Eudora was gracious in her critique but warned him against using such phrases.[119]

One Christmas vacation, Chessie noticed that Eudora had grown pale and thin. After Eudora returned to school, Chessie mailed her vitamins. Eudora fed her heavy heart in other ways. She traveled to Chicago, where she ambled along the breezy streets in her possum coat. Browsing through the shops, she thought there must be more than the cold of Wisconsin.

> *What you look for in the world is not simply what you want to know, but more than you want to know and more than you can know— better than you had wished for. Sometimes something draws you to a discovery, and there is no other happiness quite the same.*[120]

Eudora left Wisconsin still clinging to the dream she had when she arrived: to be an author. In the summer of 1929, she returned to Jackson, where she wrote for the *Daily News*. She also joined the Junior Auxiliary, although her sights remained on the one place she longed to be: New York City.

Jackson friend Leona Shotwell eventually got Eudora to New York. She called Eudora, pleading, "If you will go to Columbia University with me, Aunt Mary will let me go."

That fall, Eudora and friends Aimee Shands, Mary Frances Horne and Leona Shotwell left for Columbia University. They

roomed together at Johnson Hall. Eudora concentrated on courses in advertising and typing, which her father encouraged. He was against fiction, telling Eudora, "It's not the truth about life." He felt Eudora would be wasting her time. He wanted to be sure that she had something solid to fall back on.[121]

More Jackson friends found their way to New York through other routes. Lehman Engel had a fellowship to Julliard. Frank Lyell attended graduate school at Columbia. Also living in New York were Jacksonians Joe Skinner and Norma Long. Norma married a Yazoo

COLLEGE YEARS: THE JOURNEY

City fellow, Herschel Brickell, past editor of the *Jackson Daily News*. The Brickells often invited Eudora and the other girls over for dinner.[122]

In New York, Eudora saturated her time with the Metropolitan Museum of Art. She attended Broadway shows, including all-day Saturday shows, from ten o'clock in the morning on. On occasion, Frank snuck into the theater during intermission. He mingled with Eudora in the crowd before heading back to watch the second act without a ticket. In Harlem, she frequented the Cotton Club and Small's Paradise. She also explored Greenwich Village, where Lehman lived. To remind Eudora of home when the New York ground was snow and ice, Chessie mailed her boxes of camellias.[123]

New York now felt like home. Here, Eudora's dreams and future lay. She set out to find employment. Sadly, fate forced her into another direction—back south, to Jackson, Mississippi. Her father was dying of leukemia. It was 1931.[124]

Eudora watched her father die. Her mother, Chestina, lay on a cot beside her father. A tube ran from her arm into his as the doctors attempted a blood transfusion. This was a last attempt to

treat his leukemia. Eudora watched her mother. Chestina watched her husband. She hoped to save his life as he had saved hers years ago. This was an era ignorant to blood types and the importance of matching donors. As Chessie's blood ran into Chris's vein, mixing with his blood, he died.

While Eudora had been away from home, first at the W and then in Wisconsin and New York, Chessie developed her home landscape with arbors and trellises. There were flowering shrubs, oaks and pines and red cedars on each side of an ornamental bench. Other benches about the yard became favorite places to sit and rest or to take photographs. She kept a garden journal. She read books on house and garden, learning to develop continuity between the two. When home on college breaks, Eudora worked with Chessie in the yard. She saw how her mother enjoyed the garden experience and became educated in horticulture. Wanting a parade of bloom in the border, Chessie filled the gaps between the growing seasons of perennials with annuals. She refused to force plants to grow in environments where they could not thrive. She believed that "the gardener grows up to his garden and thus does the garden continue to be satisfying though never perfect."[125]

Before Chris's death, the garden had been a joy for Chessie. She became an artist, designing and implementing those designs on their Pinehurst lawn. In 1928, their home won the prize for "best entire place," out of twenty-five houses. The newspaper article described that her garden, "which lies at the back of the house and is entered through an arched gateway, is so much a part of the natural beauty of the place that one scarcely notices the transition from lawn to garden."[126]

After her husband's funeral, Chessie labored tirelessly in her gardens. She worked most days tending her flower gardens, planting, weeding, watering and dividing. She kept a daily record and studied books to learn the names and species, the genealogy and cultivation. Rising at dawn with her mother, Eudora moved behind Chessie in the borders. In the garden, her mother learned how to keep things alive, how to nourish the red clay of Jackson to make it productive. Chessie chose flowers that survived and flourished in normally fruitless ground. No experience taught Eudora more about grief or flowers. Nothing taught her more about achieving survival by going, fingers in the ground, and the limit of physical exhaustion. Though grieved by the loss of her husband, just as Chessie brought life to her garden, the garden resuscitated her. She gradually resumed her life with friends, neighbors and the garden club she co-founded in January 1931.[127]

The country was at the beginning of the Great Depression, but Eudora was able to find work. Her first paid job was in communications, working part time at WJDX Radio, the station her father founded, located beneath the big clock on the roof of the Lamar Life building. She edited the *Lamar Radio News*, the radio program schedule. She wrote scripts and feature articles on the local talent appearing on the air. Working also for a local paper, in addition she wrote a society column for the *Memphis Commercial Appeal*.[128] She turned to photography, thinking it might lead to more employment. Her love for photographs, of course, began with her father. His Eastman camera had a bellows that pulled out and exposed the picture by pressing a little bulb. From her father, Eudora learned that a good snapshot stopped a moment from running away. Every feeling waits on its gesture.[129]

However, writing was her passion, something she wanted to do outside Mississippi. She applied for work at Charles Scribner's Chicago office for "a position in a publishing house which will serve toward stimulating and finding a field for" her own writing. She also sent applications to Maxwell Perkins in New York and to a New York magazine, *Bookman*. All turned her down.[130]

While the Depression inched on, stuck in Jackson, Eudora and her friends longed for the artistic scene they had experienced in New York. They improvised the New York artistic culture at their get-togethers. Sometimes they held their events in the clubhouse Walter and Edward had built as boys. To entertain themselves, they dressed up and threw dinner parties. The girls wore long dresses. Everyone portrayed "somebody" in society, such as those featured in *Vanity Fair*. Eudora and friends Helen Lotterhos, Margaret Harmon and Ann Long took humorous photographs of one another imitating famous "women of fashion." The group played games like charades and word games. They took photos of one another dressed in costumes and satirized the advertising industry. To Eudora, advertising felt too much like sticking pins into people and making them buy what they did not need or want.[131]

To earn extra money, Eudora photographed fashion layouts for Oppenheimer's Store. Later, she did the same for the Emporium. Both were popular stores in Jackson. Eudora posed the models like those in *Vanity Fair*, at various locations in Jackson, including the capitol. In spite of the economy, Eudora traveled as much as she could afford to New York to try to find work. She once stayed for six weeks and applied at the *New Yorker* and *National Geographic*, with no luck. Her dreams, it seemed, were shattered from every direction.[132]

Before her father's death, the entire country felt the effects of the Depression. Over forty million people faced poverty. African Americans were the last hired and the first to be fired. Thus, they struggled even harder to find ways to make ends meet. People left their homes to find work in other cities. This made them even more destitute. Due to lack of legal residency, they were denied

College Years: The Journey

government relief.¹³³ In Mississippi, under Governor Bilbo's administration, the Depression struck in the late 1920s. Those employed in non-farming work environments began losing their jobs. Farmers, however, knew how to survive off the land. They were more able to provide their families with the bare necessities, like food and shelter. However, they faced foreclosure on mortgages they could not pay. Many were forced to become tenants and sharecroppers. In light of the growing unemployment rate, bank failures and state deficits, farmers also faced falling cotton prices. Plus, a drought caused a massive crop failure.

The 1930 census showed an increase of 12 percent in Mississippi's population, mostly in rural areas. The white population grew by 17 percent. The black population grew by only 8 percent. The state government's operational budget was at a deficit of $13 million. Debt amounted to over $50 million. This meant that the state was unable to repair the Old Capitol, which housed nine agencies that helped people. There was no funding for teachers and schools.¹³⁴ Added to this, births were increasing, and deaths were decreasing.

Jackson produced the "One Cent Plan." The plan asked its residents to donate one cent to a general fund. This allowed the city to hire and pay unemployed men and women. Due to this One Cent Plan, Jackson was able to plant sixteen community vegetable gardens to provide food for the needy. The money allowed workers to make general repairs throughout the city. Edward Welty built a duplex on a vacant lot next door to the Pinehurst house for extra income. Chessie taught bridge lessons and took in a boarder, Frances Cook. Everyone called her Fannye. A naturalist and conservationist, Fannye fit right in. Her vocation sometimes had odd things associated with it. One time, the Weltys kept a dead owl in the refrigerator until Fannye could dissect it.¹³⁵

By 1934, the Civil Works Administration (CWA) had been established in every county of the state. This administration provided approximately fifty-eight thousand jobs for people constructing and maintaining roads and bridges and improving waterways. The Federal Deposit Insurance Corporation (FDIC) ensured federally insured bank accounts. The Civilian Conservation Corporation (CCC) provided jobs toward the construction of parks and the improvement and maintenance of roads and forests. The Agricultural Adjustment Administration (AAA) furnished subsidies to farmers, helped finance new conservation methods and stabilized prices. The Rural Electrification Administration (REA) supplied electric power to many underserved areas of the state.

The social and cultural activities of the Works Progress Administration (WPA) encompassed projects of historical surveys, art, music, theater and writing. A third of its employees were women. One of these women was Eudora Welty.[136]

Traveling through and exploring her own state opened Eudora's eyes to people and places beyond her sheltered home life. Mississippi took her beyond the Broadway lights of New York City and beyond her own race and social status. This journey steered her toward the characters she would create and the stories she was destined to write.

Chapter 10
WPA, the Depression and World War II

Destination

Out of an office in the Tower Building in Jackson, Eudora worked as junior publicity agent. She worked under Louis Johnson, the senior publicity agent for the Works Progress Administration. He wrote the news. Eudora wrote feature stories and conducted interviews.[137] Now in her mid-twenties, Eudora traveled to almost every county in Mississippi. She talked to people on newly opened projects and farm-to-market roads, at juvenile court systems and airfields that had been hacked out of old pastures. Participating in library work, she rode along on the bookmobile route, distributing books. She set up booths at county fairs, staying nights at the country-town hotel. Under a loud electric fan, she wrote up the projects for the county weeklies. Her work was mostly geared toward journalism, but she started taking her camera to towns she visited—courthouse towns like Canton, Yazoo City, Tupelo, Forest and Meridian. In these places, everyone came to town on Saturdays. She used a Kodak model and developed her film at the local Standard Photo Company in Jackson. She purchased a second-hand enlarger from the State Highway Department and constructed a contact-print frame to use at home in her kitchen.

The entire country struggled through the Great Depression. Still, Mississippi had long been impoverished and devastated. The

The Inspiring Life of Eudora Welty

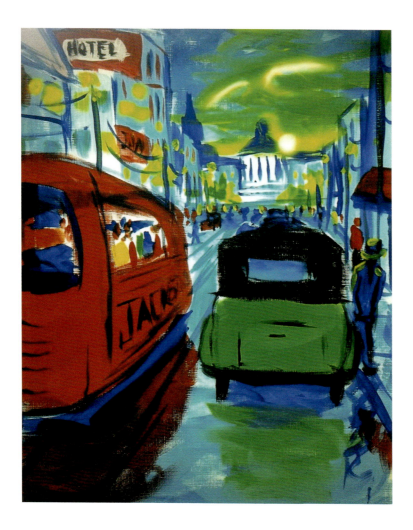

W had exposed Eudora to Mississippi's different cultures, accents and customs. Even so, she had never witnessed the immense poverty in her home state. She had always lived in two-story houses, first on North Congress and then on Pinehurst. They were comfortable homes, built of sturdy wood and brick on well-kept lawns, with tall glass windows shaded by drapes and shades. Shelves were filled with books, whatnots and instruments. Fireplaces kept her warm in the winter. Sleeping porches offered relief from summer heat. Driving dusty rural roads, Eudora came across tiny dilapidated shacks where large families lived. These poorly constructed shanties of old weathered wood quivered unsteadily on their rocky dirt lots.

Through her photographs, Eudora preserved the Depression and its stark reality. She did it in a way that spoke of the people and their circumstances. Within their faces lie meaning and confusion. Rather than posing her subjects, Eudora urged them to continue what they were doing. She wanted to capture the moments honestly, as they experienced them. She did so to expose their courage and perseverance in hopeless situations, not to mock their way of life or hardships due to poverty. She waited for the moment of authenticity, the connection with the lens. When it happened, she snapped the photo.[138]

> *The human face and the human body are eloquent in themselves, and a snapshot is a moment's glimpse into what never stops moving, never ceases to express for itself something of our coming feeling. Every feeling waits upon its gesture. Then, when it does come, how unpredictable it turns out to be, after all.*[139]

Somewhere in the Mississippi Delta, on the porch of a shanty, she saw four African American children. One stood and leaned against the shanty. Two crouched together on the rickety porch. One sat on the bottom step. In front, on the edge, sat a man leaning against a post, his legs dangling off the porch. Above his head, freshly washed clothes dangled from a clothesline. Underneath the porch, within the crawlspace, a rusted washtub sat alone. Each individual gazed out at an unseen destination. Maybe it was someone coming in from the field. Maybe the sun was dipping into the horizon and casting fiery colors into the sky. Whatever the case, the destination was left to the viewer's imagination. All that mattered was the realness of the people.

Passing remote farmhouses, Eudora often noticed the bottle trees. Some flashed alone in a field. Others nestled among a gathering of trees. One in the midst of a peach orchard caught her eye. On every limb was a blue milk of magnesia bottle or a pop bottle of orange and green, and they sparkled brightly against the sunlight. This tree later resurfaced from her memory. She placed it in her

story titled "Livvie." The fictional eye sees in, through and around what is there. Eudora brought many of her memories into being in the form of a story.[140]

Eudora did not think her photographs special. She felt they expressed life in a time when no one knew much about Mississippi. In her early years, Eudora had not even known the Delta was north of her.[141]

For only $100, Eudora could take the train from Jackson to New York and stay for three weeks. At the train station in Meridian,

WPA, THE DEPRESSION AND WORLD WAR II: DESTINATION

she waited for her New York train. Usually she read to pass the time, but the lights in the station were too lofty. For two hours, she watched one sole attendant, an old African American lady wearing a frilled bonnet and white apron. The attendant offered the waiting passengers coffee from an enormous black iron pot. From the darkness of 2:00 a.m., a distant whistle penetrated the walls of the station. The attendant began to call out the list of destinations—Birmingham, Chattanooga, Bristol, Lynchburg, Washington, Baltimore, Philadelphia and New York. The clamor of the engine, the clanging bell, the spewing steam became louder as the train rolled up to the platform. People rose and assembled. As Eudora did, she watched the attendant gather up as many suitcases as she could carry. She guided everyone to the waiting train. Remembering the fortitude of this individual, Eudora later placed her in her story called "The Demonstrators." Her spirit showed up in many others.[142]

The round-trip train fare from Jackson to New York cost Eudora about $17.50. At her stop in Washington, she purchased an additional round-trip fare from New York to Washington for $3.50. When she arrived at Penn Station in New York, she waved that ticket in the air. She sold it to the first taker, who got a good deal, and Eudora made a little profit. For $9.00 a week, she stayed at the Barizon, a grim little hotel for women only. Men weren't even allowed in the mezzanine. Though cheap, the hotel provided a free breakfast. She attended the opening of the African American *Macbeth*, set in Jamaica rather than Scotland. Put on in Harlem, it was directed by Orson Welles. The main character, Hecate, played by a black man, danced naked to the drums on stage. This impressed Eudora.[143]

The Depression in New York painted scenes of long lines of people waiting for food. Some sold apples in Union Square. Others read the daily want ads. The Depression also painted homelessness, people sleeping in clumps in subway stations, snuggled close to keep warm. Eudora photographed a mass of people rather than individuals to reveal the magnitude of plight in the big city.[144]

In New York, she also had another mission: to find a publisher for her stories. She went from office to office, leaving her manuscript on the desk. She expected to hear an answer by the end of day. When she didn't, she stayed a little longer, leaving the manuscript here or leaving it there—with no luck. She left the pictures she had taken working for the WPA at publishing houses along with her stories. Still, there was no response.

Then she took her photographs to a small gallery called Lugenes on Madison Avenue. They liked her photographs and decided to do a show there.[145]

Photography taught Eudora about coming upon people she did not know. She appreciated being allowed into scenes of other people's lives. Still, she had to go on to fiction from photography because it "was the only way she could part the veil between people—not in images but in what comes from inside in both subject and writer."[146] She wrote everywhere—on trains and in motels. All she needed was privacy. Often, the way to obtain privacy was to leave home. The anonymity of a motel provided a good place to write. The earlier it was, the better she wrote.

When Eudora had to set up a WPA booth at a carnival, she rose early to catch and photograph the workers setting up the tents and rides at the fairgrounds. Walking the fairgrounds, she drank coffee with the people working the midway. She listened to stories about sideshow acts. One story was about a small African American person who was carried off to the carnival against his will. This affected her greatly. In response to this story, she wrote another story. Because she didn't know enough about the real person, she created a fictional character. His name was Little Lee Leroy. A crippled black man, he was kidnapped into carnival work and forced to become "Keela, the Outcast Maiden." Eudora wrote the story in 1938. It was published in 1940.

Little Lee Leroy is on his porch early one summer morning, listening to the screech owls down in the woods where his daughters pick plums. Two white men, Steve and Max, trek up the path from the highway. They are looking for the person who had once been painted red and wore a red dress as Keela the Outcast Maiden. At the carnival, Keela was ordered to eat live chickens and bite off their heads while mumbling and growling like an animal. Steve "was the one cause for it goin' on an' on an' not bein' found out—such an awful thing."[147] In his own guilt and his own words, Steve remembers "how the drums was goin' and I was yellin', 'Ladies and gents! Do

WPA, the Depression and World War II: Destination

not try to touch Keela, the Outcast Indian Maiden—she will only beat your brains out with her iron rod, and eat them alive!'"

The character in the story that brings about change was a frowning man, tallish, with sort of a white face. He bought a ticket everyday to see Keela, the Outcast Maiden. One day, he wandered up to Keela. He ignored Keela's waving iron rod and everyone's warnings: "'Git away, git away,' and Keela growlin' and carryin' on an' shakin' its iron bard like they tole it to."

The man laid open his hands like a friend would do. Keela let go of the iron bar, grabbed the man's hand tightly and cried like a baby. The man said, "Do you wanna get out of this place, whoever you are?" And "it" held on to the man's hand, wouldn't let loose. The man said, "Well, wait here till I come back." The man came back with the sheriff and took everyone to jail.

Writing this story, Eudora exposed how racism is as grotesque as a carnival sideshow. She made a political and moral statement. Racism dehumanized and oppressed.[148] Eudora was still with the WPA when it disbanded with the reelection of Franklin Delano Roosevelt.[149]

Childhood friend and prolific writer Hubert Creekmore, whose sister, Mittie Elizabeth, married Walter Welty in 1939, suggested that Eudora send her stories to *Manuscript*, a small literary magazine. She submitted two stories, "Death of a Traveling Salesman" and "Magic." The journal accepted both, making these her first accepted stories for publication. Eudora thought, "Is that the way it happens? You just put something in the mail and they say okay?" She discovered luck had a lot to do with it.[150]

The larger magazines rejected her stories. With the rejections came encouraging notes, such as: "We like your story but we don't think it's right for us at this time." In fact, Eudora Welty received enough rejection slips to cover a wall. She chose not to take the rejections to heart. Instead, remembering the editors' encouraging words, she kept writing.[151] Her first published short story, "Death of a Traveling Salesman," opened her eyes to what her real subject would always be: human relationships. Daydreaming had started her on the way, but story writing, once she was in its grip, took her and shook her awake.[152]

The Inspiring Life of Eudora Welty

On October 25, 1938, from 961 America Street, Baton Rouge, Louisiana, author Katherine Anne Porter wrote to Eudora. She said that Ford Madox Ford, head of the fiction department of Dial Press, had asked her for suggestions on new candidates for publication. Katherine wrote:

> *I thought of you first, with the admirable short stories. It seems to me that if you have no other plans and have a book length collection of stories, it was an excellent idea to write to Ford, giving him some notion of your manuscript. He will then no doubt ask to see it.*[153]

Eudora heeded Katherine Anne's advice and sent her stories. Ford did indeed try to place Eudora's short story collection with a New York publisher. None was interested. They all wanted novels.

John Woodburn of Doubleday Publishing searched out new talent. He traveled to Jackson, where he called Eudora and explained the intent of his visit. Eudora picked up Woodburn from his hotel and brought him to her home. Chestina prepared waffles as John read Eudora's stories. He took the stories back with him to New York but could not place them with publishing houses anywhere. He contacted someone who could: Diarmuid Russell.[154]

> *May 28, 1940*
> *Dear Miss Welty:*
> *John Woodburn of Doubleday's* [sic] *has suggested that I write to you to see if you might need the services of an agent. I suppose you know the parasitic way an agent works taking 10% of the author's takings. He is rather a benevolent parasite because authors as a rule make more when they have an agent than they do without one. We ourselves are quite new but we have the good wishes of many of the publishers who have offered to send us all their authors without agents. Their feeling is that there are few good agents in New York and that these few are too large to be able to extend any editorial assistance, we hope to be able to do this.*
>
> *I myself have been in literature for a long time being the son of an Irish Author (A.E.). I have been sub-editor on journals and*

WPA, THE DEPRESSION AND WORLD WAR II: DESTINATION

worked in bookstores and for a couple of years was editor in a New York publishing house.
If you should need the services of an agent we was [sic] glad to help. If you are in New York I hope you will call to see us.
Yours sincerely
Diarmuid Russell (AaA, Michael Kreyling)

For the past five years, Eudora had taken her stories and photographs in person to New York to search for a publisher. She appreciated small literary journals like *Manuscript, Southern Review, Prairie Schooner* and *River*. Her desire and hope was still on larger magazines. If she was to be published in more than regional quarterlies and magazines, she needed an agent.

"Yes! Be my agent," she immediately replied to Diarmuid's letter.

On her way to the Bread Loaf Writers Conference, founded in 1926 and sponsored by Middleburg College, Eudora made a stop in New York to meet Russell and others in the agency. Eudora stayed the weekend with Russell and Rosie.

"You get all these stories back in from the folds and send them to me," Diarmuid told her.

Katherine Anne Porter had recommended Eudora for the Bread Loaf Conference. Also in attendance that year were Carson McCullers, whom Eudora could not tolerate, and John Ciardi, who had just turned twenty-four. A photo was taken of the Bread Loaf group, which included Director Ted Morrison, Marian Sims, Carson McCullers, Eudora Welty, John Ciardi, Brainard Cheney, Edna Frederickson and Louis Untermeyer.[155] Other famous authors who attended Bread Loaf included Robert Frost (known as the godfather of Bread Loaf), Ralph Ellison, Truman Capote, Sinclair Lewis, Richard Wright and more.

Diarmuid became the break Eudora needed. He labored endlessly for Eudora because he believed in her stories. Belief was the only reason Diarmuid Russell took on any story from any author.[156] He handled all Eudora's contracts for books and short stories. In particular, he became her most trusted friend. After two years, Diarmuid managed to get Eudora's work into national magazines. The first was the *Atlantic Monthly*, which accepted "Powerhouse" and

"A Worn Path." From there it was *Harper's Bazaar*. Other national magazines followed. In addition, Diarmuid worked out a contract on a collection of Eudora's short stories entitled *A Curtain of Green*. Editor John Woodburn persuaded his publisher, Doubleday, to accept the book on Diarmuid's terms. Woodburn wrote to Eudora, saying, "I knew when I tasted your mother's waffles everything would turn out all right."[157]

Katherine Porter played a huge role in Eudora's invitation to Yaddo in Saratoga Springs. Yaddo was a writers' colony founded in 1900 by Spencer and Katrina Trask. They held the colony in their fifty-five-room, gray-stone mansion on a five-hundred-acre spread with four lakes. The invitation arrived in May 1941. Eudora happily accepted. During the two months she was there, she built many friendships.[158] Woodburn traveled to Yaddo. He visited Eudora and asked Katherine Anne Porter to write the introduction to *A Curtain of Green*. She agreed. *A Curtain of Green* was published in 1941, one month before the attack on Pearl Harbor.[159]

Unable to attend the release party, Katherine Anne wrote:

> *Dear Eudora: Be happy and gay at your coming out party and remember me just enough to console me a little for not being there. All the good luck and the reward in the world to you. You deserve everything. I hope to see you there or here before you go home. With my love Katherine Anne.*[160]

This was just the beginning of Eudora's success. "The Robber Bridegroom" was published in 1942, "The Wide Net in 1943," "Delta Wedding" in 1946 and "The Golden Apples" in 1949.

The Depression had affected Eudora greatly, both as an individual and as a writer. She would never see Mississippi or her country in the same light again. However, it was Pearl Harbor and World War II that shocked her most as an artist. She was at a friend's wedding on the day of Pearl Harbor, December 7, 1941. The world forever changed. Brothers Edward and Walter, her childhood friend and sweetheart John Robinson and every other man and boy she knew marched off to war. Walter went to Okinawa. Many others went to Normandy and Italy.

WPA, THE DEPRESSION AND WORLD WAR II: DESTINATION

Diarmuid wrote to Eudora:

> *I think myself all this great war has come about because people and governments all over the world have refused to see and have even denied the existence of a world spirit.*[161]

Eudora wrote back:

> *What the war has done to the people this time I believe will be more powerful than what the people can do in marking the war, if that could be a physical fact. But it is true, it must be, that it is the outrage to the world spirit that you mention that we feel above the viciousness of each single thing and all seems to be in the solemn shadow of this violation—no, in the shadow of this spirit to which the violation is done, which is still as powerful as ever and in being denied is the more irrevocably defined. All this must take place in each heart—how strong our heart must be that nothing has ever been too much.*[162]

When Eudora later asked her brother, "How close have you come to a Kamikaze?" Walter answered, "Close enough to shake hands."[163]

During the 1940s, Eudora met author and Nobel Prize for Literature recipient William Faulkner in Oxford while she was staying with Miss Ella Somerville. Ella threw a dinner party, and Faulkner was one of her friends who attended. In 1943, Faulkner wrote Eudora a letter, saying, "You're doing real good." He asked if he could help her in any way.

"I had sent it bragging to a friend in Oxford to read," she later explained in an interview, "one of the group who knew William Faulkner, not Miss Ella."

When the friend discovered the letter years later, she sold it to the University of Virginia for a "horrendous sum," said Eudora. Eudora asked the university, "Doesn't it belong to me?"

Unfortunately, the letter now belonged to the Commonwealth of Virginia. It sent Eudora a carbon copy. Eudora framed it and hung it in the room where she worked.[164]

For a year, from 1949 to 1950, Eudora traveled extensively throughout Europe on a Guggenheim Fellowship. She had previously applied for the same fellowship in 1940, without success. All the credit for her newfound success she gave to Diarmuid Russell.[165] Along with her luggage, she carried her Rolleiflex to take photographs. On this trip, she met Elizabeth Bowen, the author of *The Last September*, *The Hotel*, *The House in Paris* and *The Death of the Heart*. Even though they had never met before, Bowen requested that Eudora come to her ancestral home, Bowen's Court, in southern Ireland so she could meet Eudora. In the mid-'40s, before Bowen met Eudora, she had given "Delta Wedding" a positive review in the publications *Tatler* and *Bystander*. She also reviewed and gave Eudora's "Golden Apples" rave reviews in England for *Books of Today* in 1950.

Eudora took the ferry to Ireland. First she went to Dun Laoghaire and then to Dublin. She walked in the country, on little roads. She ran under a hedge when it rained. "I just wanted to see it for myself, just to be there. I love Dublin," said Eudora. When she met Bowen, Eudora thought she had the best analytical mind of a writer, about writing, that she'd ever come across. Intelligent and beautiful, Bowen was tall and large boned. Her hair was the color of copper.

After Eudora's visit at Bowen's Court, she returned to Paris. She spent her May Day departure day in Meudon. She enjoyed the company of sculptor Aristide Mian; his wife, American writer Mary Mian; and their three daughters in the Mians' home. A bittersweet day of happiness and goodbyes, Eudora snapped many photographs of her friends and the memories they made. At the metro station, Eudora sat waiting on a bench. Her Rolleiflex beside her, there were also the beautiful lilacs, presents and party food the Mians had presented her before she left. As her train approached, she hurriedly gathered her gifts to board. Only after the train took off did she realize she had left her camera behind on the bench. She took the next train back to retrieve the camera, but it was gone. She grieved over the loss of recorded moments among friends who would never gather again. She punished herself by refusing to buy another camera. Her life as a photographer ended.[166]

WPA, THE DEPRESSION AND WORLD WAR II: DESTINATION

The University of Chicago and North Carolina College for Women both offered Eudora teaching jobs. Eudora had never liked the idea of teaching. She replied that "as a teacher, she was a zero." She also turned down the opportunity to teach at a writer's conference. She felt she needed to work on her writing.

Harper's Bazaar accepted her story "The Burning," about the Civil War and the defeat of the South. "The Burning" won an O. Henry award. Nonetheless, Eudora later admitted to author and historian Shelby Foote that "The Burning" was the worst story she ever wrote. The truth was that Eudora Welty felt nothing but horror and infinite regret about the Civil War. It had caused tremendous loss of life. She never read *Gone with the Wind*. Her mother's and father's people were on both sides of the war. Eudora claimed to be half southern, half Yankee. She compared what happened in the South to what had happened in Irish author Elizabeth's Bowen's home in Ireland during Cromwell's destruction. After all these years, physical memories of the Civil War remained visible in the South. This made forgetting quite impossible. Mississippi had been a battlefield. Families lost everything. Communities had to be rebuilt.

> *There was nothing, nothing, nothing to start with…It took the flower of the whole country, North and South.*[167]

Elizabeth Bowen visited Eudora in Mississippi. She formed a close bond with Chestina, unlike Katherine Anne Porter, whom Chestina disliked. After Elizabeth returned home in 1951, Eudora traveled first to London and then on to Bowen's Court, where she worked on the story "The Bride of the Innisfallen." She celebrated her forty-second birthday there.

Eudora's first correspondence with *New Yorker* editor William Maxwell on August 19, 1946, was not to encourage publication of her work. Instead, she wrote to encourage acceptance of John Robinson's work "Landlady in Algiers." Maxwell thanked Eudora for "discovering a natural New Yorker writer."[168] It was a several years before Eudora submitted "The Bride of the Innisfallen," her favorite story, to the *New Yorker*.[169]

111

The Inspiring Life of Eudora Welty

> *June 6, 1951*
> *Dear Eudora:*
> *I love your train story* ["The Bride of the Innisfallen"] *beyond all possibility of telling you. I loved it so much, while I was reading it, that I could hardly bear to pass it on to the next reader...*
> *Affectionately Bill*[170]

This was her first story published in the *New Yorker*. The magazine, however, was just as adamant about gaining first rights to Eudora's story "Ponder Heart." Harcourt would publish it as a novel in 1954, after the *New Yorker* serialized it in 1953. Nash Burger remembered a character much like Eudora's Daniel Ponder back in the early days of Jackson. His name was Wiley Cooper. He climbed the bandstand at Smith Park to make speeches, imitating the politicians at the podium. He watched and commented on tennis matches. Sometimes he ended up at the Baptist church, where he sang robustly and testified aloud.[171] For "Ponder Heart," Eudora received a $5,000 advance from Harcourt. She received $7,700 from the *New Yorker*. She also received $4,000 for the Book of the Month Club, half of which went to Harcourt. Eudora was doing quite well as an author.

> *July 20, 1953*
> *It really is just marvelous news and dazzles my head when I try to think about it till I'm sure I've taken it on. It was a feat you did—for sure—I'm more pleased than anything that it worked out exactly as it came to you it might. I can believe you did it better than I can believe what it was. It was a double feat—and do not be cast down even the least if it is not triple, that's getting too miraculous—this is miraculous now.*[172]

"Ponder Heart" garnered the interest of those in theater, including Herman Levin. Mr. Levin produced *Call Me Mister* (1946) and *Gentlemen Prefer Blondes* (1949). In 1956, he produced the London and New York versions of *My Fair Lady* (1956). In New York, Eudora's friend Lehman Engel worked in theater as a composer, conductor and co-producer. He told Eudora that Levin was an astute producer. However, Lehman, who was fond of the story, said there would have

WPA, THE DEPRESSION AND WORLD WAR II: DESTINATION

to be help on the dialogue.[173] By January 6, 1954, when *Ponder Heart* was published, Henry Volkening mailed the option agreement with Levin to Eudora for her signature. Levin had agreed to a six-month option at $500 per month. *Ponder Heart* the novel did much better financially than *Ponder Heart* the play, which deviated drastically from the book. Neither Eudora nor Russell had a say in the play.

> *That script does sound dismaying and I guess is several versions later than the one I saw months and months ago. I was told the boys were on the slapstick side and it sounds as if they were outdoing themselves—and I guess all one can do is to look grim and bear it...*[174]

Ponder Heart ran on Broadway in New York from February 16, 1956, to June 23, 1956. Una Merkel, who played Edna Earle Ponder, won the Antoinette Perry (Tony) Award for Best Featured Actress in a Play. Ben Edwards was nominated for a Tony for scenic design.[175]

Eudora found more pleasure, however, in the Jackson Little Theatre's October 1956 version of *Ponder Heart*. Staged by Eudora's friend Charlotte Capers, Capers also played Edna Earle. On opening night, Eudora, wearing a corsage, sat along with Chessie, Walter and his family in a reserved row of the theater.[176]

From February 2 to 10, 1959, the Jackson Little Theatre also produced *Cat on a Hot Tin Roof*, one of Tennessee Williams's Pulitzer Prize–winning plays. This Broadway production had played to a full house at the Morosco in New York, next door to the Music Box, where *Ponder Heart* was playing.[177] Eudora never met Tennessee Williams. While attending the W in Columbus, Mississippi, the birthplace of Williams, many stories surfaced about the Williams family. Eudora and her friends attended the *Cat on a Hot Tin Roof* performance while in New York.[178] For the Jackson performance, Eudora wrote notes on *Cat on a Hot Tin Roof* in *The Spotlight* program:

> *Mr. Williams' plays burst in on us with such extraordinary voltage that—just as after a crisis in real—we find it hard to describe afterwards what hit us. Was it violence or excruciating tenderness, that sharpest moment? Was it unbearable crudeness or extraordinary*

> *delicacy that finally drove the point home? ...Behind every play he's written we seem to hear crying out a belief that as human beings we do not go so far—no matter how far we do go—as to tell each other the truth.*[179]

In a later interview, longtime friend Charlotte Capers said this about Eudora:

> *I think she's almost beatified in Jackson. Jackson is so proud of Eudora and she is such a nice and friendly person. Jacksonians, along with Mississippians, have a terrible inferiority complex—they feel that everything in the world people say about them is bad and they have the feeling somehow that everything she's saying about Mississippi is good and funny and true. Where Faulkner didn't give a damn, and his writings were difficult, her personal popularity and the feeling of gratitude that she has represented us so well—we need this, and we're grateful for it.*[180]

Epilogue

Eudora Welty Day on May 2, 1973, felt like a dream where unexpected things turn up. Many of Eudora's friends from all over the country showed up for this one eventful day in her life. Charlotte Capers called it the day the lights went on Mississippi, the day the lights went on in the Old Capitol.

First, Eudora read from her novel *Losing Battles* in the House of Representatives at the Old Capitol.

Begun in 1955, the novel took Eudora fifteen years to complete. Sickness had plagued Eudora's family. Chessie was recuperating from cataract surgery. Walter suffered from rheumatoid arthritis. Tending to her mother and brother and managing the household consumed Eudora's time and energy.

She wrote to Diarmuid on May 28, 1957: "Haven't done any work yet (story) but am about ready to get it out…" Then, on June 26, 1957, she wrote:

> *So I have no excuse at all for not working now that the doctor-going schedule is reduced and all seems under control better. I'm so ashamed of not producing anything. I should think all my friends would have given me up. So I hope I'll be sending you this thing before too long. I've cut it some.*

Epilogue

Diarmuid wrote to Eudora on June 5, 1958:

> *Do hope things will go right so that you can get some work done. It's a long time (more than three years since "The Bride of the Innisfallen") and being what you are you will always be doing things for other people. But I do think that somehow you ought to reserve some time for yourself and your own work. Bill Maxwell and others have been talking to me about this I must say I do agree—and at this point I think others should be doing something for you, to make you freer (is that right or should it have a third E).*

Walter died a year later. Since Eudora was not publishing anything, there was very little money. Certainly, there was no money to hire a professional to assist in the care of Chessie.

On July 15, 1960, Diarmuid wrote:

> *I keep thinking of you all the time, sad that you are having such a wretched timed of it—and yet nothing for anyone to do, as far as I can see, I still feel strongly you ought, willy nilly to set aside time to write, something your own—but this, I know depends on circumstances and one's feelings…*

Chessie and Edward died within days of each other in 1966. Diarmuid was concerned about Eudora and her "battles" in her life. They, too, would certainly interrupt her work on *Losing Battles*. In fact, her work on *Losing Battles* was interrupted, but not the way Diarmuid feared. In 1967, Eudora put aside the novel to write a long short story entitled "The Optimist's Daughter." The *New Yorker* published it in 1969. *Losing Battles* would finally be published in 1970.[181]

Losing Battles was set in the hill country of Tishomingo County, Mississippi, during the Depression. The characters are uneducated and very poor. They have nothing but themselves. These characters evolved from the people and places Eudora saw while traveling with the WPA. To Eudora, battles being lost seemed much more important when there was so little left to lose. She strived to uncover her characters through their words and actions.[182] In an interview about *Losing Battles*, she said, "I needed that region, that kind of

Epilogue

country family, because I wanted that chorus of voices, everybody talking and carrying on at once." In addition to fighting battles, the title, *Losing Battles*, signified how some battles can never be won. Storms, soil erosion, drought, the Depression are all elements beyond human control, much like the deaths of Eudora's loved ones.[183]

Eudora had originally meant for *Losing Battles* to be a long story. She told an interviewer, "As the people became dearer to me—it changed."

Most of Eudora's stories hung in her mind for a long time before she set out to write them.[184] When asked about the conspicuous absence of African Americans in this story, she said:

> *I do not think that there's anything missing or anything avoided, there at all. However, Northeast Mississippi is not a part of the state where there ever were any black people because it is too poor. There were not plantations where you had sharecroppers and a society like that. There are small, independent, poverty-stricken, white, red clay hill farmers up there, and Negroes never went there. All the same,* [there is] *a very telling and essential incident in* Losing Battles *that involves an African American. Perhaps you remember.*[185]

The incident Eudora mentioned was when the story's character Uncle Nathan admitted to killing a man with a stone's blow to the head. Then, he let an African American, who worked at the sawmill, be hanged for the crime. This one powerful sentence exposed the dark truth about justice in the South during that period.[186]

After Eudora's reading at the Old Capitol, Governor Waller awarded her a "Distinguished Mississippi" plaque. She then received her fans and signed autographs in the Archives and History Building. There, her old manuscripts and letters from friends like John Woodburn and samples of her photographs were displayed as exhibits.

That night was a performance of *Ponder Heart* at the New Stage Theatre. Eudora had helped form this theater in 1965 with Jane Reid Petty, Patty Carr Black and other charter board members. Eudora never marched on Washington, nor did she organize voter registration. Her work and her actions supported interracial casts at New Stage Theatre from its planning stages. This clearly indicates

Epilogue

her belief in civil rights for all. Her story "The Demonstrators," published in 1966, prompted Jesse Jackson's praise in a letter to the *New Yorker*. The story was "true and powerful," he wrote.

Eudora had not been able to attend the opening of New Stage Theatre on January 25, 1966, due to her mother's death on January 21. She then faced Edward's death on January 26. Nonetheless, her support for the theater and its mission never waned, regardless of bomb threats from white supremacists. The open-door policy to all New Stage Theatre productions never faltered. Regular interracial casts began in 1969. Thus, New Stage was the first group in Mississippi to have interracial casts and audiences besides academic institutions. In 1970, when the State Highway Patrol and Jackson Police killed two people at Jackson State University, the Jackson State University student cast in *Ponder Heart* continued her role in the production at New Stage Theatre regardless of the danger during this turbulent civil rights period.[187]

Following the production of *Ponder Heart* on the night of the Eudora Welty Day celebration, Mr. and Mrs. Arnold Turner hosted Eudora's party in their home on Crane Boulevard.

On May 7, 1973, Frank Hains at the *Daily News* called Eudora. When she answered, he asked something like, "Well, how does it feel?" Eudora had no idea what he was talking about. She looked out her window and saw two strangers coming up the walk with a camera.

She asked, "Frank, what's happened?"

Frank had seen the news come over the AP wire. Eudora had won the Pulitzer Prize for *The Optimist's Daughter*. Originally, a short story, Eudora had expanded and published it as a novel in 1972, after the publication of her book of photographs, *One Time, One Place*, in 1971.[188]

On May 8, 1973, at Charlotte Capers's house on Berkley Drive in Jackson, Eudora shared the good news. In Charlotte's interview, she asked Eudora if this book was her most autobiographical work:

> Well, all my books are autobiographical in that I never have made up the feelings in them. I think that you have to experience emotion before you write about it…but in the case of The Optimist's Daughter, I did draw on some of the childhood and early married experiences of my own mother.

Epilogue

Had writing *The Optimist's Daughter* helped Eudora deal with her own emotions in losing her mother?

> *I think it did; although, I did not undertake it for any therapeutic reasons, because I do not believe in that kind of thing. I believe in really trying to comprehend something. Comprehension is more important to me than healing.*[189]

Epilogue

Eudora once admitted that she never stopped to think about how lucky she had been. She took publication as just a matter of course, sending stories off without any modesty or worry at all. "It's only now when I look back on it, that I'm simply amazed. Because I was very, very lucky. I didn't know enough to be scared."[190]

During the 1980s, Eudora Welty deeded her home to the State of Mississippi to become a literary house museum administered by the Mississippi Department of Archives and History. The organization that struggled so greatly to survive in the beginning had persevered and thrived through the efforts of so many, including Dunbar Rowland and Charlotte Capers. At the 1987 Faulkner and Craft of Fiction conference in Oxford, Mississippi, included was a special commemorative stamp dedication to William Faulkner. Nearly nine hundred people were in attendance. Eudora Welty was one of the speakers. She read her story "Why I Live at the P.O." Then she spoke about Faulkner:

> *Let us imagine that here and now we're all in the Old University Post Office and living in the twenties. We've come up to the stamp window to buy a two-cent stamp, but we see nobody there. We knock and then we pound, and we pound again and there's not a sound back there. So, we holler his name and at last here he is. William Faulkner. We have interrupted him. Postmaster Faulkner's treatment of the mail could be described as offhand, with a strong local tradition and some soul who still can personally remember that during post office hours when he should have been putting up the mail and selling stamps at the window up front, he was out of sight in the back—writing lyric poems. He was a postmaster who made it hard for you in general to buy a stamp or send a letter or get your hands on any of that mail that might come to you. Faulkner the Postmaster called it quits here in 1924. Faulkner the poet was able to move on with pen into his vast prose world of Yoknapatawpha County.*[191]

In 1994, thanks to Susan Haltom, the archives and a volunteer force, the renovation of Chessie's gardens at the Welty home on Pinehurst Drive began.

Epilogue

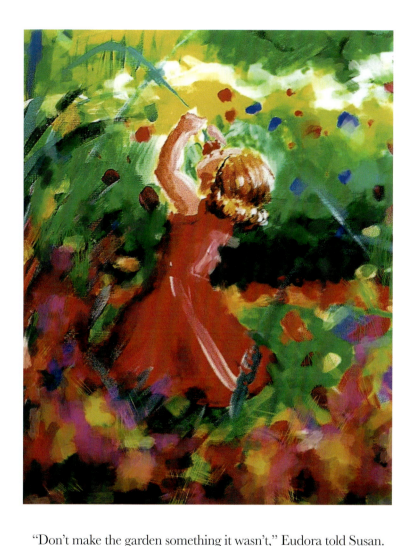

"Don't make the garden something it wasn't," Eudora told Susan.

Eudora's letters and Chessie's garden notebooks were not yet available through the archives. They relied on Eudora's memory and photographs for the replanning of the gardens. After Eudora's death on July 23, 2001, her nieces, Mary Alice and Elizabeth, found Chessie's garden records. These included diagrams and garden images. Full restoration of the gardens began with the re-creation of trellises, arbors and Walter and Edward's clubhouse. The gardens opened to the public. In 2004,

Epilogue

the Eudora Welty house and gardens were declared a National Historic Landmark.[192]

Eudora Welty's life, work and home would be open to all—forever.

> *The events in our lives happen in a sequence of time, but in their significance to ourselves they find their own order, a timetable not necessarily—perhaps not possibly—chronological.*[193] *It is our inward journey that leads us through time—forward and back, seldom in a straight line, most often spiraling. Each of us is moving, changing with respect to others. As we discover, we remember; as we remember, we discover.*[194]

Timeline

1879	Christian Webb Welty is born.
1883	Chestina Andrews Welty is born.
1904	Christian Webb Welty and Chestina Andrews Welty marry.
1907	The Weltys' son Christian Welty dies at age fifteen months.
April 13, 1909	Eudora is born in Jackson, Mississippi, at 741 North Congress Street.
1912	Brother Edward Welty is born.
1915	Brother Walter Welty is born.
1924	A sister is stillborn.
1925	Eudora graduates from Jackson's Central High School.
1925–27	Eudora attends Mississippi State College for Women, Columbus, Mississippi.
1927–29	Eudora attends and graduates from the University of Wisconsin, Madison.

Timeline

1930–31	Eudora attends Columbia University School of Business.
1931	Christian Webb Welty dies.
1931–34	Eudora works in Jackson at WJDX radio station.
1933–35	Eudora writes Jackson society columns for the *Memphis Commercial-Appeal*.
1936	Eudora publishes her first stories, "Death of a Traveling Salesman" and "Magic," in *Manuscript* magazine, has a one-woman photographic exhibit in New York City and works for the Works Progress Administration.
1937–39	Eudora publishes ten stories in the *Southern Review*, *Prairie Schooner* and *River*.
1939	Eudora works for the Mississippi Advertising Commission.
1940	Diarmuid Russell becomes Eudora's agent.
1941	Eudora publishes stories in the *Atlantic Monthly* and *Harper's Bazaar*. Her first book of stories, *A Curtain of Green*, is published.
1942	"The Robber Bridegroom."
1943	"The Wide Net."
1944	Eudora works for several months as a copyeditor and staff reviewer for the *New York Times Book Review*.
1946	"Delta Wedding."
1949	"The Golden Apples."
1949–50	Eudora travels through Europe on a Guggenheim Fellowship.
1951	Eudora spends a few months in England and Ireland.
1952	Eudora is elected to the National Institute of Arts and Letters.

Timeline

1954	Eudora lectures at Cambridge University in England and publishes *Ponder Heart*.
1955	"The Bride of the Innisfallen." Eudora receives the Howell's Medal from the Academy of Arts and Letters.
1956	Jerome Chodorov's and Joseph Fields's dramatization of *Ponder Heart* runs on Broadway.
1959	Eudora's brother Walter dies.
1963	Eudora publishes "Where Is the Voice Coming From?" in the *New Yorker*.
1966	Eudora's mother, Chestina, and her brother Edward die.
1966	"The Demonstrators" appears in the *New Yorker*.
1969	"The Optimist's Daughter" appears in the *New Yorker*.
1970	Eudora publishes *Losing Battles*, a novel begun in 1955.
1971	Eudora's book of photographs, *One Time, One Place*, is published, and she is elected to the American Academy of Arts and Letters.
1972	*The Optimist's Daughter*, in revised and expanded book form, is published. Eudora receives the Gold Medal for Fiction from the National Institute of Arts and Letters.
1973	*The Optimist's Daughter* receives a Pulitzer Prize.
1974	Eudora travels through Italy and France.
1976	Alfred Uhry's dramatization of *The Robber Bridegroom* runs on Broadway.
1978	"The Eye of the Story."
1979	Eudora is an artist-in-residence at the British Studies Program, Associated Colleges of the South, held at Oxford University.

Timeline

1980	*The Collected Stories of Eudora Welty*. Eudora receives the Presidential Medal of Freedom.
1983	Eudora delivers the William E. Massey Sr. Lectures in the History of American Civilization at Harvard University.
1984	*One Writer's Beginnings*. Eudora travels to England and Italy.
1986	Eudora receives the National Medal of the Arts.
1989	*Photographs*.
1990	Eudora travels to London
1991	*Norton Book of Friendship*, co-edited with Ronald A. Sharp
1996	Eudora receives the French Legion of Honor in a ceremony held at the Old Capitol Museum in Jackson.
1998	The Library of America publishes two volumes of Eudora's fiction and nonfiction, making her the first living writer whose works have become part of this distinguished series.
2001	Eudora Welty dies on July 23.

Resource: The Eudora Welty Foundation, http://eudorawelty.org/life-works/timeline.

Learn More About
Eudora Welby

EXCERPTS FROM INTERVIEWS WITH
EUDORA WELTY

Linda Kuehl (1972): Are you an eavesdropper?
Eudora Welty (EW): Well, in the South, everybody stays busy talking all the time—they're not sorry for you to overhear their tales. I don't feel in helping myself I ever did anything underhanded. I was helping out.

Alice Walker (1973): Has it ever been assumed that because you were born and raised in Mississippi your black characters would necessarily suffer from a racist perspective?
EW: I see all my characters as individuals, not as colors, but as people, alive—unique.

Jean Todd Freeman (1977): Do you consider that you had a normal kind of a childhood?
EW: It's always been a family full of curiosity and interest in the world.

Learn More About Eudora Welty

Jan Nordby Gretlund (1978): Was there a tradition of storytelling in your family?
EW: Yes, on my mother's side they were big storytellers. When her brothers came here to visit, they would renew the stories of their youth, funny things that happened in West Virginia out in the country. They grew up on a farm. Every name they mentioned would bring out gales of laughter and reminiscences—there would be songs: "Remember how we used to sing…?" So they would all sing.

Louis D. Rubin Jr. (1979): When you took those pictures in 1935 or 1936, did you have the sense at the time that you were preserving something?
EW: Oh, no indeed not. I took them because something appealed to me in the form that a story or an anecdote might have—to capture something. I did it for the moment.

Patricia Wheatley (1986): What sort of influence did your father have on you in terms of your work?
EW: Cautionary, probably, because he knew I was pretty venturesome. I think I probably shot off a good deal in writing things for the school paper and all, and he tried to curb this in me…He wanted me to be sure that I knew what I was talking about—a good, good rule.

Hermione Lee (1988): Do any of your stories come out of the photographs you took in the Depression years in Mississippi?
EW: I am an observer and I would notice the same thing…But I didn't make up stories from my pictures. The odd thing is that some of the photographs turned out almost to illustrate stories that I wrote later.

Clyde S. White (1992): You took a lot of summer trips with your parents…how did they affect you as a fiction writer later on?
EW: Well, they just fed my love for story. Stimulated it…In those days there were hardly even any maps to be had down there. They used the AAA automobile blue Book, which told you how to get somewhere. There weren't too many signposts…

Learn More About Eudora Welty

We were so adventurous. You never knew what was going to be around the corner.

Leslie R. Myers (1984): Your childhood is so interesting to read about; why do you think that is?
EW: I don't think I was so different as a child. Our day was different. We were readers. We didn't have television. Traveling was different from today; you were conscious of the countryside. Now you're not conscious of the countryside. Now you just get on a plane and get off.

Eudora Welty to Susan Haltom and Jane Roy Brown before the restoration of Chessie Welty's gardens on Pinehurst Drive: I cannot bear to look out the window and see what has become of my mother's garden…That was a happy time, when the garden was new. We used to have…[Eudora stopped]. *That is a sad phrase.*

Resources:
Haltom, Susan, and Jane Roy Brown. *One Writer's Garden.* Jackson: University of Mississippi, 2011.
Prenshaw, Peggy Whitman, ed. *Conversations with Eudora Welty.* Jackson: University of Mississippi, 1984
———. *More Conversations with Eudora Welty.* Jackson: University of Mississippi, 1996.

What Others Have Said about Eudora Welty

Perhaps the best example of the polished craftsman among [those who have made their names during and since the last war] *is Miss Eudora Welty.*
—*"The Art of the Short Story," in* American Writing Today, *edited by Allan Angoff (New York: New York University Press, 1957): 188–90.*

Learn More About Eudora Welty

At thirty-four she is frequently heralded as the most powerful of contemporary short-story writers.
—*"Before Band Wagons,"* Vogue, October 1, 1943.

Between her sketch writing, completion of a new novel called The Golden Apples *and absorption in the career of Danny Kaye, Eudora is busier these days than a relief pitcher for a tail-end ball teams.*
—Bennett Cerf, *"Trade Winds,"* Saturday Review of Literature 32 (May 28, 1949): 4.

She was not the contentedly cloistered "Miss Eudora" in whom so many believed or wanted to believe, but was someone far more passionate and compelling: a woman and a writer with a "triumphant vulnerability."
— Suzanne Marrs, Eudora Welty, a Biography *(New York: Harcourt, Inc., 2005).*

Although Welty quite clearly regards some aspects of a writer's private life as properly belonging to him or her, not to be offered up to anyone with a question and a tape recorder, she is characteristically gracious and surprisingly forthcoming in taking on questions that are personal as well as professional.
—*Peggy Whitman Prenshaw, ed.*, Conversations with Eudora Welty *(Jackson: University Press of Mississippi, 1984).*

Her stories teach us nothing directly except, through her vision, how to observe, and wonder and love, and see the mysteries; for brutal or lovely, they wait for us wherever we go.
— Ruth M. Vande Kieft, Eudora Welty *(Boston: Twayne Publishers, 1987).*

Notes

Prologue

1. Ann Waldron, *Eudora: A Writer's Life* (New York: Doubleday, 1998), 303; Peggy Prenshaw, ed., *Conversations with Eudora Welty* (Jackson: University Press of Mississippi, 1984), 120.
2. Reynolds Price, "One Writer's Place in Fiction," July 27, 2001.
3. Sarah Brash and Loretta Britten, eds., *The 60s: Turbulent Years, Our American Century* (Alexandria, VA: Time Life, Inc., 1998), 23–37, 46, 63–73.
4. Harold Bloom, *Eudora Welty: Bloom's Bio Critiques* (New York: Chelsea House Publishers, 2004), 54–56.
5. Prenshaw, *Conversations*, 31.
6. Harriot Pollack and Suzanne Marrs, eds., *Eudora Welty and Politics: Did the Writer Crusade?* (Baton Rouge: Louisiana State University Press, 2001), 75–78.
7. Suzanne Marrs, *Eudora Welty, a Biography* (New York: Harcourt, 2005), 151, 186.
8. Darlene Harbour Unrue, ed., *Katherine Anne Porter Remembered* (University Alabama Press, 2010), 135.
9. Walter Clemmons, *New York Times Book Review*, April 12, 1970; Prenshaw, *Conversations*, 32.
10. Waldron, *Eudora*, 316; Marrs, *Eudora Welty*, 275, 320, 353.
11. Marrs, *Eudora Welty*, 355.
12. Robert L. Gale, *A Ross Macdonald Companion* (Westport, CT: Greenwood Press, 2002), 248.

13. Eudora Welty, *A Writer's Eye: Collected Book Reviews* (Jackson: University Press of Mississippi, 1994.
14. Marrs, *Eudora Welty*, 357–61.
15. Suzanne Marrs, ed., *What There Is to Say We Have Said: The Correspondence of Eudora Welty and William Maxwell* (New York: Houghton Mifflin Harcourt, 2001), 279.
16. Marrs, *Eudora Welty*, 386.
17. Michael Kreyling, *Author and Agent: Eudora Welty and Diarmuid Russell* (New York: Farrar, Straus and Giroux, 1991), 208.
18. Ibid., 209.
19. Eudora Welty, *One Writer's Beginnings* (Cambridge, MA: Harvard University Press, 1984), 68. Hereafter cited as *OWB*.
20. Ibid., 104.

Chapter 1

21. *OWB*, 47.
22. Ibid., 97.
23. Ibid., 47.
24. Ibid., 25.
25. Ibid., 47.
26. Ibid., 9.
27. Ibid., 62–67.
28. H.A. Wheeler, "The St. Louis World's Fair," Official Guide of the St. Louis World's Fair, Office Guide Company, http://www.1904worldsfairsociety.org.

Chapter 2

29. John Ray Skates, *Mississippi's Old Capitol: Biography of a Building* (Mississippi Department of Archives and History, 1990), 68, 92–93; Julie Kimbrough, *Jackson*, Images of America (Charleston, SC: Arcadia, n.d.).
30. Westley F. Busbee Jr., *Mississippi, A History* (N.p.: Harlan Davidson, Inc., 2005), 170–72, 178.
31. Mississippi Department of Archives and History (MDAH), Lamar Life Insurance records, mdah.state.ms.us/manuscripts/z1851.html; Kimbrough, *Jackson*.
32. *OWB*, 17–18.

Chapter 3

33. Marrs, *What There Is to Say*, 64.
34. *OWB*, 10.
35. Ibid., 17–18.
36. Eudora Welty, *Photographs*, selected and edited by Patti Carr Black (Jackson: University Press of Mississippi, 1989), 20, 27.
37. *OWB*, 5.
38. Ibid., 34.
39. Ibid., 35–36.
40. Ibid., 4.
41. Ibid., 3–4.
42. Ibid., 6.
43. Ibid., 4–5.
44. Ibid., 10.
45. Peggy Prenshaw, ed., *More Conversations with Eudora Welty* (Jackson: University Press of Mississippi 1999), 122.
46. *OWB*.
47. Prenshaw, *More Conversations*, 141.
48. *OWB*.
49. Ibid.

Chapter 4

50. *Mississippi's Old Capitol*, 125–27.
51. "Long Boy," a World War I ballad.
52. Busbee, *Mississippi: A History*, 205–10; Paul Mathless and Loretta Britten, eds., *1910–20: End of Innocence, Our American Century* (Alexandria, VA: Time Life Inc., 1998), 24–29, 132–38.
53. Kimbrough, *Jackson*, 19, 20, 21.
54. MDAH, Lamar Life Insurance records.
55. *The Eye of the Story* (New York: Random House, 1978); "The Little Store," 1975, 11, 22–25.
56. *OWB*, 11.
57. *Eye of the Story*, 328.
58. Prenshaw, *More Conversations*, 42; "Looking into the Past: Davis School," interviews with Davis School alum Eudora Welty, writer, October 7, 1980.

59. "Looking into the Past."
60. *OWB*, 22–25.

Chapter 5

61. Busbee, *Mississippi*, 213–15.
62. http://www.nps.gov/malu/forteachers/jim_crow_laws.htm.
63. Prenshaw, *More Conversations*, 14–15; *OWB*, 14.
64. Ibid., 13.
65. Ibid., 53.
66. Ibid., 61.
67. Ibid., 64–65.
68. Ibid.
69. Ibid., 20–21.

Chapter 6

70. Busbee, *Mississippi*.
71. *OWB*, 29–30.
72. Ibid., 9.
73. Ibid., 26–27; Patti Carr Black, ed., *Early Escapades* (Jackson: University Press of Mississippi, 2005), 18.
74. Black, *Early Escapades*, 10.
75. http://flyingdreams.home.mindspring.com/nick.htm.
76. Prenshaw, *Conversations*, 205.
77. Prenshaw, *More Conversations*, 123.
78. *OWB*, 33.
79. Ibid., 39.
80. Ibid., 30.
81. Ibid., 73.
82. Ibid., 10.
83. Bob Batchelor, *The 1900s* (Westport, CT: Greenwood Press, 2002), 66–68.

Chapter 7

84. Nash Burger, *Mississippi Writers: Reflections of Childhood and Youth* (Jackson: University Press of Mississippi, 1995), 18.

85. Black, *Early Escapades*, 45–59.
86. Burger, *Mississippi Writers*, 19.
87. Ibid.
88. *One Writer's Imagination: The Fiction of Eudora Welty* (Baton Rouge: Louisiana State University Press, 2002), 4 (hereafter cited as *OWI*); Susan Haltom and Jane Roy Brown, *One Writer's Garden* (Jackson: University Press of Mississippi, 2011), 44, 50.
89. Prenshaw, *More Conversations*, 16; Black, *Early Escapades*, 12; Marrs, *Eudora Welty*, 11–12.
90. Eudory Welty, "The Whistle" (New York: Doubleday, Doran and Company, 1941).
91. *OWI*, 3.
92. Marrs, *Eudora Welty*, 14)
93. Haltom and Brown, *One Writer's Garden*, 23–25; Marrs, *Eudora Welty*, 14–15; Waldron, *Eudora*, 20–21.
94. *OWB*, 45.
95. Haltom and Brown, *One Writer's Garden*, 24–25.
96. Ibid., 49.

Chapter 8

97. Paul Mathless and Loretta Britten, *The '20s: The Jazz Age, Our American Century* (Alexandria, VA: Time Life Books, 1998), 32–33, 35.
98. Black, *Early Escapades*, 10, 11.
99. Marrs, *Eudora Welty*, 15–16.
100. Black, *Early Escapades*, 12.
101. Haltom and Brown, *One Writer's Garden*, 21.
102. Nash Burger, *The Road to West 43rd Street* (Jackson: University Press of Mississippi, 1995), 37.
103. Black, *Early Escapades*, 16–17; Waldron, *Eudora*, 12; Burger, *Road to West 43rd*, 36.
104. Burger, *Road to West 43rd*, 36.
105. Black, *Early Escapades*, 18.
106. Marrs, *Eudora Welty*, 16, 17.
107. Haltom and Brown, *One Writer's Garden*, 21.
108. Marrs, *Eudora Welty*, 16; Waldron, *Eudora*, 23–24.
109. Black, *Early Escapades*, 20.

Chapter 9

110. *OWB*, 77–80.
111. Black, *Early Escapades*, 20.
112. Waldron, *Eudora*, 23–33; *OWB*, 76-81; Marrs, *Eudora Welty*, 17–18; Black, *Early Escapades*, 22–26.
113. Waldron, *Eudora*, 40.
114. *OWB*, 80.
115. Ibid., 81.
116. Waldron, *Eudora*, 37.
117. Marrs, *Eudora Welty*, 20–21.
118. Kreyling, *Author and Agent*, 10.
119. Waldron, *Eudora*, 28; Marrs, *Eudora Welty*, 21–22; letter from Burger to Welty, May 23, 1929, MDAH, Welty Collection.
120. Marrs, *Eudora Welty*, 21–22; Waldron, *Eudora*, 36; Kreyling, *Author and Agent*, 10–11; Black, *Early Escapades*, 52.
121. Prenshaw, *Conversations*, 146–47; Waldron, *Eudora*, 43.
122. Waldron, *Eudora*, 44–45; Black, *Early Escapades*, 31–34.
123. Prenshaw, *More Conversations*, 291.
124. Marrs, *Eudora Welty*, 27–29.
125. Haltom and Brown, *One Writer's Garden*, 32–33, 37, 95.
126. Ibid., 51.
127. Ibid., 67, 69.
128. Ibid., 103; *OWB*, 84.
129. Prenshaw, *Conversations*, 98; *OWB*, 84–85.
130. Marrs, *Eudora Welty*, 40; Waldron, *Eudora*, 42–43.
131. Haltom and Brown, *One Writer's Garden*, 103; Welty, *Photographs*, xxi.
132. Haltom and Brown, *One Writer's Garden*, 103; Marrs, *Eudora Welty*, 39.
133. Sarah Brash and Loretta Britten, *The '30s: Hard Times, Our American Century* (Alexandria, VA: Time Life, Inc., 1998), 42.
134. Skates, *Mississippi Old Capitol*, 134.
135. Haltom and Brown, *One Writer's Garden*, 102, 103)
136. Busbee, *Mississippi*.

Chapter 10

137. Prenshaw, *More Conversations*, 207.
138. *OWB*, 85.

139. *One Time, One Place* (New York: Random House, 1971), 12.
140. OWB, 85.
141. Prenshaw, *Conversations*, 155; Harriet Pollack, *Eudora Welty, Whiteness and Race* (Athens: University of Georgia Press, 2013), 41; *Eye of the Story*, 354, 355; Welty, *Photographs*, Exiii-xxviii; Prenshaw, *Conversations*, 146.
142. OWB, 94–95.
143. Prenshaw, *Conversations*, 146, 218.
144. Prenshaw, *More Conversations*, 194.
145. Prenshaw, *Conversations*, 145–47.
146. Prenshaw, *More Conversations*, 151.
147. Eudora Welty, "Keela, the Outcast Indian Maiden" (New York: Doubleday, Doran and Company, 1941).
148. Pearl Amelia McHaney, *Occasions: Selected Writings* (Jackson: University Press of Mississippi, 2009), 177.
149. Prenshaw, *Conversations*, 158.
150. Prenshaw, *More Conversations*, 292.
151. Prenshaw, *Conversations*, 344, 345.
152. *OWB*, 87.
153. Unrue, *Katherine Anne Porter*.
154. Prenshaw, *Conversations*, 41–42.
155. Edward Cifelli, *John Ciardi: A Biography* (University of Arkansas, 1997), 64.
156. Prenshaw, *More Conversations*, 22.
157. *OWB*, 97.
158. Unrue, *Katherine Anne Porter*, 135.
159. Michael Kreyling, *Understanding Eudora Welty* (Columbia: University of South Carolina Press, 1999).
160. Unrue, *Katherine Anne Porter*, 96.
161. December 26, 1941.
162. Late December 1941.
163. Prenshaw, *More Conversations*, 66, 162, 266)
164. John Griffin Jones, *Mississippi Writers Talking: Interviews with Eudora Welty, Shelby Foote, Elizabeth Spencer, Barry Hannah and Beth Henley* (Jackson: University Press of Mississippi, 1982), 11–12; Carol Kort, *A to Z of American Women Writers*, 348.
165. Marrs, *Eudora Welty*, 159.
166. Pearl Amelia McHaney, *Eudora Welty, the Contemporary Reviews* (Cambridge, UK: Cambridge University Press, 2010); Harold

Bloom, *Eudora Welty* (New York: Chelsea House Publishers, 2004), 43–44; Prenshaw, *More Conversations*, 101–02, 196–97.
167. Prenshaw, *More Conversations*, 120–21; 112–14; Waldron, *Eudora*, 212–13.
168. Marrs, *What There Is to Say*, 23.
169. Waldron, *Eudora*, 226.
170. Marrs, *What There Is to Say*, 26.
171. Waldron, *Eudora*, 231; Burger, *Road to West 43rd*, 38.
172. Kreyling, *Author and Agent*, 167–68.
173. Ibid., 169.
174. Ibid., 178.
175. *Montreal Gazette*, "Merkel Dies at 82," January 6, 1986.
176. Marrs, *Eudora Welty*, 262; Waldron, *Eudora*, 250.
177. Waldron, *Eudora*, 247–48.
178. Patricia Grierson, *Mississippi Quarterly*, September 22, 1995; Prenshaw, *More Conversations*, Introduction xvi; Marrs, *Eudora Welty*, 250.
179. McHaney, *Occasions*.
180. Prenshaw, *More Conversations*, 4.

Epilogue

181. Kreyling, *Author and Agent*, 189–205.
182. Prenshaw, *Conversations*, 28; Haltom and Brown, *One Writer's Garden*, 108–10.
183. Ruth M. Vande Kieft, *Eudora Welty* (Boston: Twain Publishers, 1987), 152.
184. Prenshaw, *Conversations*, 30–31.
185. Ibid., 48.
186. Pollack and Marrs, *Eudora Welty and Politics*, 124.
187. Ibid., 84; Prenshaw, *Conversations*, 128.
188. Prenshaw, *Conversations*, 191.
189. Ibid., 115–16.
190. Ibid., 33.
191. Ann J. Abadie, *Faulkner and the Craft of Fiction*, edited by Doreen Fowler (Jackson: University Press of Mississippi, 1989), 215–16.
192. Haltom and Brown, *One Writer's Garden*, 213, 217, 221, 229.
193. *OWB*, 68.
194. Ibid., 102.

Collected Works

Photography by Eudora Welty

Country Churchyards. Jackson: University Press of Mississippi, 2000.
McHaney, Pearl Amelia. *Eudora Welty as Photographer.* Jackson: University Press of Mississippi, 2009.
One Time, One Place. New York: Random House, 1971.
Photographs. Jackson: University Press of Mississippi, 1989.

Writings by Eudora Welty

Black, Patti Carr, ed. *Eudora Welty's World: Words on Nature.* Jackson: University Press of Mississippi, 2005.
"The Bride of the Innisfallen" and Other Stories. New York: Harcourt, Brace and Company, 1955.
The Collected Stories of Eudora Welty. New York: Harcourt, 1980.
A Curtain of Green. New York: Doubleday, Doran and Company, 1941.
Delta Wedding. New York: Harcourt, Brace and Company, 1946.
"The Demonstrators." In *The Collected Stories of Eudora Welty*, pp. 608–22. New York: Harcourt, 1980.

COLLECTED WORKS

Eudora Welty, Complete Novels. New York: Library of America, 1998.
Eudora Welty, Stories, Essays, Memoir. New York: Library of America, 1998.
The Eye of the Story. New York: Random House, 1978.
The First Story. Jackson: University Press of Mississippi, 1999.
The Golden Apples. New York: Harcourt, Brace and Company, 1949.
Losing Battles. New York: Random House, 1970.
Marrs, Suzanne, ed. *What There Is to Say We Have Said: The Correspondence of Eudora Welty and William Maxwell.* New York: Houghton Mifflin Harcourt, 2011.
McHaney, Pearl Amelia, ed. *Occasions: Selected Writings.* Jackson: University Press of Mississippi, 2009.
———. *A Writer's Eye: Collected Book Reviews.* Jackson: University Press of Mississippi, 1994.
Morgana: Two Stories from "The Golden Apples." Jackson: University Press of Mississippi, 1988.
One Writer's Beginnings. Cambridge, MA: Harvard University Press, 1984.
On William Faulkner. Jackson: University Press of Mississippi, 2003.
On William Hollingsworth Jr. Jackson: University Press of Mississippi, 2002.
On Writing. New York: Modern Library, 2002.
The Optimist's Daughter. New York: Random House, 1972.
The Ponder Heart. New York: Harcourt, Brace and Company, 1954.
The Robber Bridegroom. New York: Doubleday, Doran and Company, 1942.
The Shoe Bird. New York: Harcourt, Brace and World, Inc., 1964.
Some Notes on River Country. Jackson: University Press of Mississippi, 2004.
Welty, Eudora, and Ronald A. Sharp, eds. *The Norton Book of Friendship.* New York: W.W. Norton and Company, 1991.
"Where Is the Voice Coming From?" In *The Collected Stories of Eudora Welty*, pp. 603–07. New York: Harcourt, 1980.
The Wide Net and Other Stories. New York: Harcourt, Brace and Company, 1943.

WRITINGS ABOUT EUDORA WELTY

Appel, Alfred. *A Season of Dreams: The Fiction of Eudora Welty.* Baton Rouge: Louisiana State University Press, 1965.

Barilleaux, Paul, ed. *Passionate Observer: Eudora Welty Among Artists of the Thirties*. Jackson: Mississippi Museum of Art, 2002.
Binding, Paul. *Eudora Welty, Portrait of a Writer*. London: Virago, 1994.
Black, Patti Carr, ed. *Early Escapades*. Jackson: University Press of Mississippi, 2005.
———. *Eudora*. Jackson: Mississippi Department of Archives and History, 1984.
Bouton, Reine Dugas, ed. *Eudora Welty's* Delta Wedding. Amsterdam: Rodopi, 2008.
Brown, Carolyn. *A Daring Life*. Jackson: University Press of Mississippi, 2012.
Desmond, John, ed. *A Still Moment*. Metuchen, NJ: Scarecrow Press, 1978.
Devlin, Albert J. *Eudora Welty's Chronicle: A Story of Mississippi Life*. Jackson: University Press of Mississippi, 1983.
———, ed. *Welty, A Life in Literature*. Jackson: University Press of Mississippi, 1987.
Dollarhide, Louis, and Ann J. Abadie. *Eudora Welty, A Form of Thanks*. Jackson: University Press of Mississippi, 1979.
Gretlund, Jan Nordby, and Karl-Heinz Westarp, eds. *The Late Novels of Eudora Welty*. Columbia: University of South Carolina Press, 1998.
Haltom, Susan, and Jane Roy Brown. *One Writer's Garden: Eudora Welty's Home Place*. Jackson: University Press of Mississippi, 2012.
Harrison, Suzan. *Eudora Welty and Virginia Woolf*. Baton Rouge: Louisiana State University Press, 1997.
Johnson, Carol Ann. *Eudora Welty, A Study of the Short Fiction*. New York: Twayne, 1997.
Kreyling, Michael, ed. *Author and Agent: Eudora Welty & Diarmuid Russell*. New York: Farrar Straus Giroux, 1991.
———. *Eudora Welty's Achievement of Order*. Baton Rouge: Louisiana State University Press, 1980.
Manning, Carol S. *With Ears Opening Like Morning Glories: Eudora Welty and the Love of Storytelling*. Westport, CT: Greenwood Press, 1985.
Mark, Rebecca. *The Dragon's Blood: Feminist Intertextuality in Eudora Welty's* The Golden Apples. Jackson: University Press of Mississippi, 1994.
Marrs, Suzanne. *Eudora Welty, A Biography*. New York: Harcourt, 2005.

———. *One Writer's Imagination: The Fiction of Eudora Welty*. Baton Rouge: Louisiana State University Press, 2002.

———. *The Welty Collection: A Guide to the Eudora Welty Manuscripts and Documents at the Mississippi Department of Archives and History*. Jackson: University Press of Mississippi, 1988.

McHaney, Pearl A., ed. *The Contemporary Reviews*. Cambridge: Cambridge University Press, 2005.

———. *Writers' Reflections Upon First Reading Welty*. Athens, GA: Hill Street Press, 1999.

Mortimer, Gail L. *Daughter of the Swan: Love and Knowledge in Eudora Welty's Fiction*. Athens: University of Georgia Press, 1994.

Pitavy-Souques, Daniele. *La Mort de Méduse*. Lyon, France: Presses Universitaires de Lyon, 1992.

Polk, Noel. *Eudora Welty, A Bibliography of Her Work*. Jackson: University Press of Mississippi, 1994.

Pollack, Harriet, and Suzanne Marrs, eds. *Eudora Welty and Politics: Did the Writer Crusade?* Baton Rouge: Louisiana State University Press, 2001.

Prenshaw, Peggy W., ed. *Conversations with Eudora Welty*. Jackson: University Press of Mississippi, 1984.

———. *Eudora Welty, Critical Essays*. Jackson: University Press of Mississippi, 1979.

———. *More Conversations with Eudora Welty*. Jackson: University Press of Mississippi, 1996.

Schmidt, Peter. *The Heart of the Story*. Jackson: University Press of Mississippi, 1991.

Trouard, Dawn, ed. *Eye of the Storyteller*. Kent, OH: Kent State University Press, 1989.

Vande Kieft, Ruth. *Eudora Welty*. Rev. ed. New York: Twayne, 1987.

Waldron, Ann. *Eudora, A Writer's Life*. New York: Doubleday, 1998.

Westling, Louise. *Sacred Groves and Ravaged Gardens: The Fiction of Eudora Welty, Carson McCullers, and Flannery O'Connor*. Athens: University of Georgia Press, 1985.

Weston, Ruth D. *Gothic Traditions and Narrative Techniques in the Fiction of Eudora Welty*. Baton Rouge: Louisiana State University Press, 1994.

About the Author

*R*ichelle Putnam has been an artist-in-residence at schools and for the Girl Scouts of America, and she has facilitated journaling sessions for various recovery groups and in prison settings with incarcerated women. She is a graduate of three Institute of Children's Literature courses, the Gotham Writers Fiction Certificate Program and the Advanced Writing Program of Open College for the Arts. A freelance writer by profession, she writes for several magazines and is the special features director for *Southern Writers* magazine. Her personal essays and fiction have been published in *A Cup of Comfort for Mothers and Daughters*, *A Cup of Comfort for Christmas Prayer*, the *Copperfield Review* and more. She is a Mississippi Arts Commission (MAC) Literary Artist and Teaching Artist and a Mississippi Humanities Council Speaker. Her nonfiction book *Lauderdale County, Mississippi: A Brief History* was published by The History Press in 2011. Her website is www.richelleputnam.net.

Visit us at
www.historypress.net

This title is also available as an e-book